The Althouse Press

Purdy: **Townshend of Huron**

By the same author:

Bright the Vision: A History of the Church of St. John the Evangelist (1988)

TOWNSHEND *of* HURON

J. D. Purdy

The University of Western Ontario

THE ALTHOUSE PRESS

First published in 1992 by
THE ALTHOUSE PRESS
Acting Dean: *B.B. Kymlicka*
Director of The Press: *D. Gutteridge*
Faculty of Education, The University of Western Ontario,
1137 Western Road, London, Ontario, Canada N6G 1G7

Editorial Assistant: Katherine Mayhew
Cover Design: Louise Gadbois, U.W.O. Graphic Services
Photo Credits: The *London Free Press* Collection of Photographic Negatives, D.B. Weldon Library, U.W.O.; Victor Aziz

Canadian Cataloguing in Publication Data

Purdy, J. D. (Judson Douglas), 1932-
Townshend of Huron

Includes bibliographical references and index.
ISBN 0-920354-33-5

1. Townshend, William A., 1898-1988. 2. Education - Ontario - London. 3. Anglican Church of Canada - Bishops - Biography. 4. Bishops - Ontario - Huron (County) - Biography. I. Title.

BX5620.T68P8 1992 283'.092 C92-093547-8

Printed and bound in Canada by The Aylmer Express Limited,
390 Talbot Street East, Aylmer, Ontario, Canada N5H 1J5

To my mother

Ethel Reid Sarah Purdy

with love

CONTENTS

Preface i

Introduction 1

1 *Student and Teacher* 7

2 *The Rector* 21

3 *The Diocesan Commissioner* 41

4 *The Crowded Years* 61

5 *The Episcopate* 91

6 *The Years of Retirement* 127

Notes 143

Bibliography 157

Index 163

Preface

This book grew out of an unusual episode. On a June afternoon in 1984 Bishop William A. Townshend presented the Townshend Gold Medal for the leading student in the graduate programme at the Faculty of Education, University of Western Ontario to a student for whom I was the supervisor. In introducing the Bishop, Professor Paul Park, then Dean of the Faculty, described some of Townshend's major contributions to education, of which I had been almost totally unaware. In a subsequent discussion with Dean Park about Townshend's life, we decided that something should be done to record this impressive career. After further reflection I decided that a biography recounting his long and active career in education and the Anglican Church of Canada would be the most appropriate vehicle.

In writing this book I have accumulated a number of debts. Dean Paul Park gave enthusiastic support and encouragement from the beginning and very generously supplied financial assistance. Three archivists at the Diocese of Huron Archives—Charles Addington, Cathy Phillips, and Diana Coates—all assisted in helping with the Townshend papers and other records in their charge. Greg Harper spent a summer as a research assistant diligently going through the files. Archdeacon A.E. Chovaz, secretary-treasurer of the Diocese of Huron, kindly permitted me to use materials at the diocesan office. The Rev. Canon Robert Foster, the Bishop's son-in-law and rector of the Church of the Redeemer, London, generously made that church's archives available. Principal Charles Jago kindly permitted me to use the minute books of Huron College Council. Mr. Ed Phelps and his staff at the Regional History Room, Weldon Library, The University of Western Ontario allowed me to use valuable source material in their depository, as did the archivists at the Ontario Archives in Toronto. Prof. R.D. Gidney, who was chair of my department while the book was being written, offered encouragement and advice.

Many members of the Townshend family were very helpful. Mrs. Robert Foster helped me unravel her brothers' and sisters' dates of birth and marriages. Mr. William Townshend and his daughter Susan lent me taped interviews they made with the Bishop in his later years. Mr. A.L. Crich of Sarnia shared his knowledge of the Bishop's family history.

I wish to thank my typist, Miss Michelle Barnes, for spending long hours wrestling with the peculiarities of my manuscript. Our departmental secretaries, Stephanie McLeod, Linda Colvin and Nicole Lombardi also helped to polish the final version. Prof. Don Gutteridge, Director of The Althouse Press, and his able assistant, Katherine Mayhew, did the editing. To my son, Sean, who watched me spend long hours reading notes and working at the word processor, I can only say thanks for your patience and understanding. I alone, of course, am responsible for any errors in this book.

J. D. Purdy

Introduction

Virginia Woolf said it best, "Yes, writing lives is the devil".[1] The English poet, W.H. Auden, labelled biographers as "gossip-writers and voyeurs calling themselves scholars".[2] Robert Skidelsky, the English biographer, claims that in England at one time it was assumed that anyone was capable of writing biography "who put half a mind to it. Indeed, half a mind was usually all the subject got, since biography, as a well-known retirement pastime, was frequently a matter of the half-dead chasing the dead."[3]

The writing of biography has rarely received enthusiastic acclaim from either literary critics or historians in the past. Until recently the former deplored the lack of any kind of theory for this style of writing as there was for poetry or fiction.[4] The views of two of England's major twentieth-century historians will suffice to underline the attitude of many of their professional colleagues. Francis West—describing the attitude of Sir Lewis Namier, the expert on English parliamentary development in the eighteenth century—claimed that Namier thought "Biographers...feared the unbounded fields of history and preferred the boundaries of a single life because they lacked creative imagination. They also lacked professional standards."[5] Discussing the views of Sir Geoffrey Elton, recently Regius Professor of History at Cambridge University, West paraphrased Elton's claim that since "no man so completely dominates an age that its history can be written in terms of him, biography should not therefore be concerned with history, except in so far as, on very rare occasions, it centres upon, or emanates from the individual whose life is being written."[6] Contemporary social historians, who try to view history from the bottom up with their computers and quantitative techniques, deplore biography as virtually a waste of time. They regard it simply as a warmed-up version of the now discredited "great man" theory of history.

These are harsh words indeed. To balance such negative assessments, Leon Edel, one of this century's consummate biographers, asserted that, "Biography is a noble and adventurous art, as noble as the making of painted portraits, poems, statues."[7] He sub-titled his book on the writing of biography *Principia Biographia*, in imitation of Newton's influential *Principia Mathematica*, with the apparent intention of compiling a set of universal rules for writing in the genre. But any such attempt would be a highly dubious undertaking and even if successful would in all probability receive less than unanimous approbation from scholars. The continued absence of theory, which, as noted, so many literary critics have deplored in the past, has recently been offset by a deluge of articles and books attempting to correct the situation. The paucity of original material drove one scholar, David Novarr, to produce a collection of statements from biographers commenting on their methodology. He titled the book *The Lines of Life: Theories of Biography, 1880-1970*.

What is one to make of this bad press? After all, the current book market is flooded with lives of the great, the near-great, and the less-than-significant. The reading public eagerly consumes stories of prominent individuals, especially if they contain salacious titbits about the private lives of politicians or Hollywood stars. There seems to be an innate thirst for knowledge about people who have been successful, however one defines success. Perhaps readers respond to Eric Homberger and John Charmley's comment that, "We learn from biography, it brings us closer to other people's lives."[8] Possibly some type of vicarious relationship is at work here.

In spite of the aspersions of modern critics, biography has an ancient lineage stretching back to the Greek and Roman historians. English biographers trace their descent from James Boswell's famous *Life of Johnson*. Nineteenth-century Victorian writers produced those ponderous and highly moralistic two-tome works which often slide dangerously close to hagiography. But it was Lytton Strachey, with his scathing attack on those same Victorian worthies in his *Eminent Victorians*, published just as the First World War was drawing to a close, who is generally credited with refashioning biography, and freeing it from the excessive moralism and lack of character analysis of that era. Strachey himself described the composing of lives as "the most delicate and humane of all the branches of the art of writing."[9]

That observation set a very high standard.[10] But composing biography is hard work. Using similar materials and techniques as the historian, the biographer must scramble about in his sources, attempting to detect his subject's personality and his relation to the currents of thought of the era. As many commentators have noted, the writer must try to delineate both the outer person, with the attendant public actions and deeds, and the inner self with its drives, demons and motivations—what Edel calls the "figure under the carpet."[11] How does an author handle this elusive inner self? Must the writer resort to some psychological theory to unravel the hidden being? If so, which school of psychology is the most useful? Does the biographer need expert training in psychology itself? Should psychoanalysis be undergone as some practitioners of psychohistory have done? Many contemporary historians and biographers have, with a limited a degree of success, used psychology in their work, but the results have not always been successful and often the critics have been unmerciful in their adjudication.[12] Some of the most critically acclaimed biographies written by Canadian historians—such as D.G. Creighton, J.M.S. Careless, William Kilbourn, Kenneth McNaught and others—have eschewed this route and still managed to present vivid word pictures of their subjects.

The search for the outer self is perhaps somewhat easier. Here the biographer needs only the paraphernalia that historians traditionally have used—letters, diaries, memos, dispatches, even laundry lists. Everything is grist for the historian's mill. As Edel correctly observed, "By its very nature biography has been wedded always—and always will be—to the document, to fact and anecdote and certainly to gossip."[13] The author simply applies the techniques of historiography to ferret out the facts and construct an interpretation of his subject's life and role in society. That statement is, of course, an oversimplification, for the process is arduous and fraught with pitfalls and traps.

THIS BIOGRAPHY, IN THE MAIN, is based upon a collection of letters and memos written by Bishop William A. Townshend during a period of almost five decades when he was an administrator in the Anglican Diocese of Huron and a trustee on the London Board of Education. Virtually all of his correspondence dealt with the business affairs of these two institutions. Yet, it can be asked, how can such a collection disclose anything about Townshend's character, his "figure under the carpet"? Some of the letters deal with the domestic affairs of the clergy, teachers and their families, and reveal Townshend as a very sensitive and humane man. Many files contain letters he sent to a myriad of friends and acquaintances who were celebrating promotions, various anniversaries, confirmations, birthdays, etc. or who were mourning the death of loved ones. Again his basic sensitivity and warm Christian charity emerge from these letters. Unfortunately he did not keep a diary. He was not an introspective type. He was too busy, too consumed by affairs to indulge in this activity.

Readers will discover that Townshend served on countless committees, which churned out volumes of reports and minutes. These, of course, are exceedingly valuable as they are the basis for making policy decisions but, like all documents, they have their limitations. Committee minutes rarely record the cut and thrust of debate. They usually state in bland fashion only the final agreement. Moreover, his service on so many committees poses a problem of selection for the historian. Which were the most significant in the long term? Not an easy task!

Edel mentioned anecdotes as a source of information. Everyone loves a good story! A man like Townshend naturally spawned dozens, if not hundreds. What does the biographer do with them? Potentially, anecdotes can be illustrative and informative about a person, but how reliable are they? They have a tendency to enlarge themselves with time and to acquire a polish, magnitude and additional detail that bear only a tenuous relationship to the original event. They can be and should be used, but with care. The first chapter is, in large part, based on a serious of taped interviews between Townshend and two members of his family. He had a remarkable memory with a phenomenal recall of events and persons. These interviews are practically the only source for his youthful years. Townshend told innumerable stories in these interviews. Delightful and amusing as many of them are, one must exercise caution in using them for these are the memories of an aged man refracted through the prism of a very long life. A measure of discretion and careful selection had to be applied. Many, regretfully, had to be omitted.

A discussion of anecdotes leads on to the use of oral history *per se*, a genre which can be as exacting as any form of historical investigation but, on the other hand, can be richly rewarding and exciting. Yet, again, as with all types of research, it has its pitfalls—the major one being a reliance on fallible human memory. Townshend delighted in telling stories about himself and others, but there was little analysis of the causes and implications of the events referred to. The anecdotes tend to supersede history; they become detached from reality. A different approach, adopted in this work, was to submit a questionnaire to retired clergy who had been associated with Townshend. Since virtually all of these men were elderly, their responses, too, required a measure of critical judgement. Yet their answers yielded some vital information about Townshend and his activities, which could then be checked against other sources.

WHY WRITE THIS BIOGRAPHY? Townshend's career, over a long span of time, had a distinct uniqueness about it. He played a role in two spheres—education and religion—which most contemporary Canadians have assumed exist as separate entities. But Townshend, for reasons explored in this book, saw it differently. His Anglican heritage precluded such a division. Life was a unity; it was not lived in water-tight compartments. Family, church and school were the nurseries of future Christian citizens. His life then presents an opportunity, rare in Canadian history, especially in the twentieth century, to view the contributions made by religion and education to the formation of Canadian society as seen through the thoughts and deeds of a man who was a player on the local, provincial and national scenes. This is not to suggest that he had the reputation or stature of a prime minister or a cabinet minister, nor did he attain the prominence accorded to the primate of the Anglican Church of Canada or even some of his fellow clerics. Nonetheless, he was an individual of considerable influence in two spheres of human endeavour, especially during the period from the early 1940s to the middle 1960s. He certainly made some significant contributions to education, where he often voiced ideas ahead of his time, and to the life of the Church. Though he was never a major contestant, he was welcomed in the corridors of power. It was "as an actor in the historical process, that [Townshends' life] assumes significance for the historian."[14]

Virginia Woolf was right!

CHAPTER ONE

Student and Teacher

Little Willie Townshend just could not wait to be born. "My mother always told me that I arrived unexpectedly, the day of the church's garden party, and that my coming really wrecked the whole show."[1] No doubt it did! One can see some of the women scurrying around searching for towels, blankets and other necessary items while others helped the mother to a house close by where she could lie down for the event. And then, suddenly there he was. What an auspicious beginning for a future cleric. Perhaps it foreshawdowed the very active life this little boy was to lead.

William Alfred Townshend, born on June 1, 1898, was the third child of Albert and Hannah (*née* Scotchmere) Townshend. He had been preceded by his brother Ernest, born in 1893, and by his only sister, Eleanor, in 1896. The Townshends went on to have two other sons, Alvin, in 1899, and John, three years later.

The Townshends were a farm family living in the prosperous agricultural area of south-west Ontario. Huron County, where Willie resided for the first 18 years of his life, had been settled in the nineteenth century largely by immigrants from the British Isles. On his father's side the Townshends had been yeomen farmers in Yorkshire, but his grandfather, another William, had decided that life in the new world might offer his family a better existence. Arriving in Upper Canada in 1847, the Townshends settled near Berlin. However, three years later William and his wife, Elizabeth, succumbed to the cholera epidemic. His third child, also named William, moved to the Bayfield area where Albert Townshend, our Willie's father, was born in 1869. He married Hannah Scotchmere in November, 1892.

The Scotchmeres were also from England. Originally this family had been merchants and shopkeepers in Bury St. Edmunds in the East Anglia area. The first Scotchmere to emigrate to Upper Canada was Alfred George, who arrived sometime between 1855 and 1860. After numerous trips back and forth across the ocean, he married Eleanor Watson and settled in Bayfield. This couple had 11 children, the eldest of whom, Hannah, became Willie's mother. Obviously there was a strong English background in Willie's ancestry, and most of his forebears had been members of the Church of England.[2]

During Willie's first six years the family moved around Huron County, living on three different farms while the father worked as a day labourer or as a carpenter. Later he became the foreman on the Forest farm near the town of Clinton, the county seat. Since the father was often absent from home, Hannah became the virtual head of the household. She was one of those strong-willed mothers who was determined that her sons would achieve positions in this world.[3] The home she and Albert provided for their offspring was full of love and warmth. Each child was regarded as a distinct personality who needed nourishing and nurturing. Both parents were typical Victorians, however, who demanded a strict accounting from their brood for all of their actions and imposed a stern discipline. In later years when he was a bishop, at the end of recounting a story about one of his youthful escapades, Townshend said: "My dear mother looked after my physical well-being, and when she got through her performance, my dad took care of my moral well-being."[4] Father Albert was never reluctant to use the strap on his sons' backsides. He kept a razor strap hanging on the kitchen wall and often told inquiring people, "Well, I want to assure you that it's just not there for an ornament. It's used whenever it's needed."[5] Albert used it quite liberally—even when the boys were in their teens—but never in a mean-spirited or vicious manner.

A sense of duty to one's neighbours, loyalty to the British monarchy and, above all, devotion to God and his church, were instilled early and constantly in the Townshend children. All during his life Willie acknowledged the powerful impact his mother's teaching and guidance had upon him. To her he always ascribed whatever success he achieved in life. The family, which included a wide network of relatives, was another source of strength and happiness to Willie and his siblings, and reinforced the values imparted by all the adults. Without intending to romanticize this situation (for the Townshends often faced difficult economic times), it is not unreasonable to suggest that this circle of relatives reflected the ideal version of the Christian family.

At the age of six, along with scores of other youngsters across Canada, Willie entered Grade 1 in a public school. He spent the first few weeks at the Clinton elementary school and then moved to the Bayfield Public School. The first day in a new school is often an exciting experience for a child, but for young Willie it was doubly so for he met a pretty, lively little girl named Kathleen Elliott. Immediately, he recognized a kindred spirit. This was a meeting which, in spite of many separations over the years, blossomed into a real romance and ultimately a marriage.

His removal to the Bayfield school led to a traumatic episode in his young life. On the first day of classes he received a severe thrashing about the head and neck from his teacher. He was literally scarred for life by this beating. Apparently the teacher thought that young Townshend had been responible for a disturbance which had actually been caused by the older lads. So severe was the beating that Willie was rendered unconscious. He was taken home, and a specialist came out from Clinton to examine him. He warned the family that the boy probably would not live for more than 48 hours. Willie, as it turned out, was not totally unconscious, and when he heard the doctor's diagnosis he said to himself that he certainly had no intention of dying.[6]

Slowly Willie recovered, but he had to stay home for two years under a doctor's care. Chaffing under this regime and being a playful, high-spirited boy, he began to take advantage of his situation by demanding an undue amount of attention. Suspecting that his son was using his illness thus, father decided that a spanking might teach Willie to be a more considerate child. But Hannah, fearing further damage to her son, persuaded his father to seek the doctor's advice first. The physician agreed with Albert's view of Willie's behaviour, and told him to go ahead and discipline the boy. Albert, never reluctant to punish misbehaviour, took the strap down from the wall and applied it to

Willie's posterior. This cold jolt of reality quickly brought the boy into line.

It was about this time that the family moved yet again: to the Murphy farm in Goderich township, several miles north of Bayfield. Although this was the farm which Willie loved more than any other, moving this distance meant leaving Kathleen behind, and that was a terrible blow. "As we went by the hardware store at Bayfield, I saw Kathleen out with some of her sisters playing. I thought that I was going to the other end of the world, and that perhaps I might never see her again, so it was a very sad heart I took with me that day to the Murphy farm....I always remember that day well, since it was on April 8, 1907, the day my wife became nine years old."[7]

After recuperatng from his injury, Willie returned to school. Even though he had missed two years, he was placed in the fifth grade. He was a bright little lad and a quick learner; but he was also a mischief-maker who was often in trouble with his teachers. Many a time he had to stay after school to write out lines or do arithmetic problems. He soon attracted the attention of his teachers, who recognized his ability and pushed him. Invariably he stood at the top of his class as he worked his way through the Ontario readers and math books, absorbing not only factual information but also the implicit values and attitudes which these books (and the teachers) imparted to generations of pupils. The school reinforced the ideas of Christian morality, patriotism and the work ethic that Willie imbibed at home. This was the heyday of the British Empire, and it could be said that these characteristics, taught to its children, had helped make it great. Moreover, all this was part of the providential order, and Willie, like so many of his school chums, was caught up in the fervent emotion of British patriotism. Indeed throughout his whole life, Townshend was to remain an outspoken champion and admirer of all things British.

In June, 1910, Willie wrote his high-school entrance examinations, that dreaded hurdle which any child in Ontario who wanted to attend secondary school in those days had to surmount. He was successful, and eagerly anticipated entering Clinton Collegiate Institute in the fall term. However, his labour was needed on the farm; and the family moved again. This time they settled on the Mason farm, just two miles north of Clinton; and because Ern, his oldest brother, had gone out west to work on an uncle's farm, Willie had to take his place at home. "I had to stay home and farm," he later recounted. "I loved farming and didn't object. They told me I would get started to high school later."[8] In the meantime, he tried to keep up his studies so that he would not fall too far behind his companions.

He spent the next four years at home. While he missed not being at school, farming made up for the loss. Willie revelled in tilling the soil, planting in the spring, harvesting in the fall, breaking in colts, tending the pigs. It was the pigs he loved! One of his greatest joys was to wallow around in the pen with them. Anyone who ever encountered Townshend in later years soon realized that this man was a true son of the soil. An abiding affection and an acute understanding of the rural way of life became a dominant feature of his character. He once told a young correspondent, "I am very proud of having been born and brought up on a good Ontario farm. One cannot get a better start in life. The training teaches you to be resourceful."[9]

Resourcefulness was only one of the many lessons he learned on the farm. Perseverance and hard work—those necessary traits of a successful farmer—were also acquired during these years. Soon he earned a reputation throughout the community as a very capable and hard-working boy, who was constantly called upon by neighbours to assist with extra chores, especially during planting and harvesting time. Yet, in spite of his deep love for farm life, he found it constricting. There was another world beyond Huron County, one that offered some fascinating challenges; and he yearned to tackle them. But he realized that he needed an education; he had to return to school. He almost did so when he turned fourteen, but once again family circumstances dashed his hopes. It was a bitter disappointment. Ultimately, however, supported by his mother and in the face of his father's strenuous opposition, Willie did eventually enter high school—in September, 1914. He was already considering becoming an Anglican priest, and so it was high time to begin preparation for this role. Moreover, his brother Ern had told him that the Elliott girls, including Kathleen, were going to attend Clinton Collegiate Institute in the fall. Here was another spur to his ambition. He just had to be there!

Willie enrolled in the collegiate just a few weeks after the outbreak of the First World War. As yet the War had not really touched the lives of most Canadians, and, besides, as everyone said, the fighting would be over by Christmas. So he entered the old building in a happy mood, and on that first day whom should he encounter but Kathleen.

> I'll never forget that first day. I looked—we all met in the assembly hall—the whole school—and I looked around for Kathleen Elliott. In fact, I looked for all three Elliott girls and I couldn't—didn't recognize one of them. So I felt very badly that I couldn't find her in the assembly hall that morning, but when we came out of the assembly hall I decided that I'd go back and as I went back, I found a very slim young lady coming out. When I had left Bayfield seven years before, she was a lovely chubby little girl and this girl was very thin and very slight. And so I thought maybe this must be an Elliott girl, so I had to say something, so I said, "I'm coming back for a pencil that I left." And she—a pencil of course which I didn't have. And she said that she had gone back to look for a handkerchief which I told her later she had never lost.[10]

There was no question but that this sprightly young girl was the long lost Kathleen. Of course, Willie was eager to court her, but decided that he had to prove himself at school first. After all, he had been away from it for four years and although he had tried to keep up his studies, he feared he was behind the other students.

The curriculum of the Ontario collegiate was a rigorous one. Even the brightest students found it hard going. Much emphasis was placed on rote learning, the drilling of essentials, and the regurgitation of material on the inevitable examinations, especially the ones written in June, upon which promotion depended. He need not have worried. Willie was a quick and apt student. He regularly stood near or at the top of his class. Actually, he completed the five years of work in four. Whether he was slogging his way through Hall and Knight's *Junior Algebra* or George Wrong's *The British Nation*, he absorbed it all. He really excelled in languages. Not only did he take French and Latin, but he was also one of two students who worked their way though White's *First Greek Book* in John Wesley Treleaven's Greek class.

As previously mentioned, Townshend's ancestors were all members of the Church of England. Moving to Canada had not changed this allegiance. Willie grew up in an Anglican home and had been baptised in Trinity Church, Bayfield. His mother was a very active church worker and taught Sunday School. According to Townshend, she was a constant Bible reader. So it was only natural that Willie would become involved in church activities. He was prepared for confirmation by Rev. C.E. Jeakins, then rector of Clinton. Jeakins, who had formerly been a professor at Huron College, possessed a charming personality and had a way with young people. He made a strong impact on young Townshend, and encouraged him to pursue his desire to enter the ministry. Another person who influenced him in these years at the church in Clinton was Fred Sloman, a school teacher, who later became famous for his railway-car school in northern Ontario. Sloman had Willie in his Sunday class, learned of his hope to be a cleric, and helped him to keep his ambition alive. In these adolescent years at St. Paul's Church, Willie became an active member of the parish branch of the Anglican Young People's Association, speaking in many of the area churches on behalf of this organization. He was getting a taste for the pulpit.

One activity which young Willie indulged in while still on the farm, and which would become an avocation in later life, was making real-estate deals. His first foray into this territory happened in 1917 when the family was offered a farm several miles north of where they were then residing. His father was reluctant to undertake this deal, but Willie begged him to let him try to arrange the financing by auctioning off some of their surplus livestock. Once again, Hannah interceded for her ambitious son, and Albert relented. On the day of the auction they raised 500 dollars more than they actually needed. The property was purchased and within a year Willie resold at a profit of 2,000 dollars.[11] Not bad for a youngster! As the years passed, Willie was to make many more real-estate deals, some of which helped to finance his university education.

These years were not entirely consumed by work and study. Willie and his siblings and friends enjoyed a very active social life.

> We had lots of fun too. We played baseball. We played football. We had a lot of football in the community. We had a field in which we had all these sports, and we also had a wonderful pond for skating. It was a little field next to the Hardy home straight north of us and there was the most wonderful skating there, that young people in the community used to gather there regularly to skate...[12]

In fact, young Townshend became quite an athlete. Baseball and football (it is not clear if this was English rugger, soccer, or Canadian football) were his favourites. He also earned a considerable reputation as a track man while at Clinton Collegiate.

By the time he finished high school, he had made a firm decision to study for the Anglican ministry. To enter this profession he needed to attend university, and for potential seminarians in south-west Ontario that invariably meant attending Huron College, the Anglican college affiliated with Western University (as the University of Western Ontario was then called) in London. He enrolled in the arts and theology programmes in September, 1918, and moved into the Huron College residence. The only sad note about this decision was being separated from Kathleen again. She would not be accompanying him; she had enrolled at the Stratford Normal School to become a teacher. The romance had developed, however, to the stage where they had decided to be married as soon as he had graduated and was ordained.

THE YOUNG MAN WHO boarded the train at Clinton that September to make his fateful journey to London already possessed many of the traits and values that were to be his constant guide and signposts throughout a long life. A photograph of him as a student at Huron College shows a healthy-looking young man with a shock of blonde hair and bright blue eyes set in a friendly, handsome face. Although he possessed a rather powerful body developed by hard work on the farm and his athletic pursuits at school, he was not, as events would show, as robust as he had thought. But his brain was sharp, and while he was not an outstanding intellect, he was always a good student. Allied with his mental and physical capabilities was a set of values acquired at home, at school, and at the parish church: honesty, temperance, the importance of hard work, and the rewards of loyalty. One was put on earth to be of service to one's neighbours. This was the cultural baggage he brought with him to London, and these were his strengths. They would serve him in times of happiness and in times of stress. Ironically, they could also be a source of weakness, for they would often prevent him from understanding some of the significant transformations that, in later years, assailed and partly undermined the world in which he had been raised. However, such ironies lay in the future.

The story of Huron College's founding and development has been told before and does not need to be recounted here. Suffice it to say that the brand of Anglicanism taught in the divinity school was low church or evangelical, particularly the Irish Anglican variety. Many of the early settlers and clergy of this region, including Bishop Benjamin Cronyn, the college's founder, were from Ireland. By the time Townshend entered its doors, Huron College, together with Wycliffe College in Toronto, had long been regarded as one of the bastions of the low-church group in the Church of England in Canada. Huron was a college where the great truths of the Protestant Reformation, as interpreted by the English Church, were emphasized. The principal was Rev. C.C. Waller, a classics graduate of Trinity College, Cambridge. Waller, a champion of the evangelical cause, had been appointed to this post in 1902, and remained there for almost 40 years. He became a power in the diocese, moulding the beliefs and practices of generations of clerics. Waller not only taught most of the theology courses at the college but was also professor of Hebrew in the university. As it turned out, this language became one of Townshend's favourite subjects.[13] Very early on, a close relationship grew up between the eager young student and the "Princ" (as Waller was nicknamed), and continued long after Townshend became a priest.

In many ways Huron College was a very closed, in-bred community in those years. Most of its students came from the same geographical region and possessed a similar type of educational and religious background. London was still a very Anglo-Saxon enclave with its sedate, comfortable, wealthy elite and its history as a one-time British garrison town. It was a conservative, flourishing small city, and like most

Canadian cities at that time was not known as a centre of intellectual or artistic life.[14] The university was also small, and lacked the stature or reputation of its rivals in Toronto and Kingston. Yet it offered its students a solid academic fare combined with the usual extra-curricular activities. For many, Western was a happy place to spend a few youthful years.

However, the War had a deleterious effect upon both the university and the college. Financial resources were hard hit, while many of the teaching faculty and student body had joined the armed services. At the beginning of the War, the college had a large enrollment but this was quickly depleted. By the time Townshend graduated in 1921, the enrollment was only one-half of what it had been in 1914.

Somehow Townshend was able to enter directly into the second year of the Honours English and History course. Furthermore, he persuaded the college officials to let him take his arts courses in the morning and his theology ones in the afternoon. This was an unprecedented step and, as a perusal of the calendars for those years indicates, this combination made for a very heavy load.[15] The arts programme demanded much reading and writing, while the divinity testamur required an intensive study of Biblical exegesis, dogmatic theology, ecclesiastical history, apologetics, Greek, Hebrew, Patristics, and a study of the *Book of Common Prayer*.

Townshend had hardly enrolled as a student when his career was almost ended. In 1918 an influenza epidemic swept the world, killing more people than did the battles of the First World War. When it struck London, the university, like other institutions, closed its doors. Townshend and most students were sent home. When the university reopened, he came down to London on the train accompanied by three girls he had known at Clinton Collegiate. Within four days all three girls died of the flu. Townshend also contracted it, and decided to go back home. His illness became so intense on the return trip that an army veteran had to take care of him and help him off the train. Years later, while conducting a funeral, he met his helper, who was now a United Church minister, the Rev. Duncan Guest. Immediately the two became lifelong friends.[16]

Seminarians were expected to assist in a parish: teaching Sunday School, helping with the services, and occasionally preaching. In fact, during his student days, Townshend preached in many churches throughout the diocese. (With his remarkable memory he could recall the names of many of these parishioners—much to their amazement—in later years when he was a diocesan administrator.) It would seem that little time was left for student antics, but it would have been uncharacteristic of him to be found on the sidelines if there was mischief afoot. He continued to play baseball and football for the college's teams. During the summer vacations he either worked on the farm or substituted for clergymen who were on holidays. In the summer of 1920 he did pastoral work in the Diocese of Qu'Appelle in Saskatchewan. While there he met a rising young lawyer named John George Diefenbaker, who became another close friend. No doubt they shared their enthusiasm for the Conservative Party and the monarchy.

The burden of these manifold activities, however, was to be Townshend's undoing. In his final year he served as student assistant to Archdeacon Richardson, the rector of St. Luke's Church, Broughdale, on the northern edge of London. When Richardson became too ill to handle his pastoral responsibilities, Townshend assumed many of them, including preparing and preaching two sermons every Sunday. The load was too much. When he sat for one of his final examinations in the spring of 1921, he collapsed from physical exhaustion and had to be sent home to recuperate. He never completed his Bachelor of Arts degree, but Huron College did grant him the Licentiate of Theology (L.TH.) diploma.

Fearing that Townshend's condition might seriously undermine his career in the church, Bishop Williams had him examined by a team of doctors. They warned the Bishop that the young man's health was precarious and that he might suffer another breakdown. Armed with this report, Williams refused to ordain him. Later, Townshend learned that Williams feared he might become a charge on the diocese's finances if he developed serious health problems. (Williams later admitted this to Townshend and was genuinely embarrassed by his decision.) Townshend got the last word on this episode when, over 60 years later, he stated, "But as I look back with some satisfaction to me, that in my

88th year I am still going and those three doctors and the examining doctor, the guys have been dead these many years. Yeah, I gotta [sic] say that."[17]

Townshend was crushed by the decision! His hopes and aspirations had been instantly dashed. For years he had wanted to be a priest; he had worked and studied hard to achieve his goal; now his future had been summarily snatched from him. What was he to do? And there was still Kathleen and their dreams. She was already a teacher. Why not follow her lead? Teaching was an honourable profession, and he had enjoyed the children in Sunday School classes. So, in the autumn of 1921, he enrolled in the model school attached to Clinton Collegiate to become a teacher. Four months later he earned his teaching certificate and was offered a contract by the trustees of the little town of Manilla, near Lindsay. He quickly accepted it. His salary was 1,200 dollars, increased to 1,600 dollars after the first four months.[18]

What should he do about Kathleen? The time had come. He proposed; she accepted. Owing to complications at her home, the young couple were quietly married in Toronto on December 23, 1921 at St. Bartholomew's Church on Danforth Avenue by the Rev. Frank Powell, another Huron graduate. After a happy feast at Kathleen's sister's apartment, the newly-wedded couple spent the night at a hotel in the city. "I'll never forget writing up the register when the clerk stuck it in front of me. I was a bit excited too, and I wrote down William Townshend and then I forgot. I realized I [had] forgotten all about my bride, and I knew I had to say something about adding a lady."[19] Perhaps both Kathleen and the clerk were surprised by that addition. They spent Christmas day with both families back in Bayfield, and then after the holidays journeyed to Manilla, where they rented rooms. The school was a continuation school, which meant that it also included the first two years of high school along with the elementary section. When the other teacher left, Kathleen was hired to take her place. She taught the younger children while he took the older ones.

THE NEXT FIVE YEARS were happy and eventful ones. They both enjoyed teaching enormously. They quickly became favourites with their students and the local community. In many ways Manilla was simply a replica of their experience back in Huron County. There was a basic rhythm and pattern to this way of life, one which had not been entirely undermined by the War. Townshend continued to be involved in real-estate deals and in the buying and selling of livestock. Both he and Kathleen became active in the Anglican parish of Lindsay; in the summer he often filled in for the rector, and preached in other Anglican churches for vacationing clergy. The couple enjoyed putting on the Christmas plays that were such an important part of the local social life.

During their stay at Manilla, the first three children were born. Eleanor, the first daughter, arrived in 1923. Their oldest son, John, was born in 1925 and he was followed by William in 1926. An amazing start had been made on a family which eventually would grow to include ten children.

Townshend also organized sports at the school for the youngsters. His baseball and track teams soon earned quite a reputation for their prowess. At a meet in Whitby he chanced to encounter the Anglican rector, the Rev. T.G.A. Wright. Wright had been a professor at Huron College during Townshend's student days. The rector, surprised at the incredible recovery in Townshend's health, immediately informed Bishop Williams of this development. Williams, in turn, contacted Townshend and offered to ordain him. But as Townshend had just signed a new two-year contract with the board, he did not accept. However, the Bishop kept the pressure on, inviting Townshend to come to London to write the deacon's examinations. Townshend finally took this step in the spring of 1926, and was made a deacon in the Church of England in Canada. He was immediately appointed to the parish of Bervie, Kingarf, and Kinlough not very far from his beloved Huron County.

He had achieved his goal.

CHAPTER TWO

The Rector

What was the state of the Church of England in Canada when Townshend was ordained? The census of 1921 indicated that this denomination was still increasing its membership. Much of the growth, however, was due to continuing British immigration, and this source was now beginning to diminish. Moreover, Canadian Anglicans had always relied upon the mother country for some of their funding and for a supply of clergymen. The First World War had made serious inroads into both of these sources. Fewer men offered themselves for ordination after the War, while the leading English missionary organizations, the Society for the Propagation of the Gospel in Foreign Parts (S.P.G.) and the Church Missionary Society (C.M.S.) found their finances seriously eroded. In 1920, the C.M.S. informed the Canadian Church that it was withdrawing its support.[1]

These trends forced the national leaders to assume more responsibility for the management of the Church's affairs. Two months before the signing of the armistice in November, 1918, the General Synod, meeting in Toronto, adopted measures to strengthen its ability to carry out the Church's mission and, at the same time, to transform the Church into a more indigenous institution. Three major departments were organized, with headquarters in Toronto. The General Board of Religious Education (G.B.R.E.), with oversight of Sunday Schools and youth work, was created. A department of Literature and Supplies was set up to assist the G.B.R.E. and parishes to obtain books, pamphlets and supplies. To co-ordinate the Church's increasing activities in the field of welfare, a Council for Social Service (C.S.S.) was appointed.[2]

General Synod accepted a Canadian version of the *Book of Common Prayer*, which now became the standard for liturgical practices across the dominion. Lastly, to offset the loss of revenues from England, Synod launched a national fund-raising campaign, known as the Anglican Forward Movement. By the time it was completed in 1924, it was a huge success. Its aim was not simply to raise funds; it also tried to teach Anglicans the value of establishing diocesan and parish budgets, and to impress upon parishioners the need to contribute regularly towards the Church's work. All in all, this synod injected a new note of efficiency and vigour into the Church's administration.

Another striking feature of Church life in these years was the upsurge of lay participation. The Women's Auxiliary (W.A.), which had been organized in 1886, witnessed a tremendous growth with branches for women of all ages being opened in parishes across the country. Units of the Mothers' Union enjoyed a similar development. Chancel or Altar Guilds to help the clergy arrange the church for Sunday services were being formed. Youth work, a somewhat neglected area of Anglican life before the War, was highlighted by the extension of Sunday Schools (and especially the novel experiment of Sunday School by post). Hundreds of Cub and Brownie packs, Girl Guide companies and Boy Scout troops appeared. But the major achievement in this area was the fostering of the A.Y.P.A. While this society had been founded before the War, it was in the 1920s and succeeding decades that it flourished, drawing in thousands of adolescents and young adults who became active A'Yers.[3] Men had always been involved in the administrative work of the Church, especially in handling the finances, but in this decade different types of clubs for them appeared as they began to diversify the roles they played in the Church's life.

And so it was a Church that appeared poised on the threshold of expansion into which Townshend was ordained. Yet, at the same time, the Church of England, as with other Christian denominations, found itself operating in a new environment. As the Canadian church historian, John Webster Grant, has pointed out,

> The changed atmosphere of the 1920s was a reflection in Canada of a process of secularization that had been affecting western civilization for centuries but was speeded up by the First World War. Canadians had been somewhat sheltered from its effects by their lack of sophis-

TOP: *BACK ROW: Left to right, Alvin, John, Eleanor, Ernest, Willy. FRONT ROW: Mother, Father.*

BOTTOM: *First picture of Willy and Kathleen, 1915, after a successful field day at Clinton Collegiate Institute.*

TOP: *Townshend (second from left) and fellow students at Huron College, 1918.*

BOTTOM: *Townshend and his famous girls' baseball team at Bervie.*

TOP: *The rector and the Rover crew at the Church of the Redeemer, London.*

BOTTOM: *Dr. Cameron Wilson, Tom Kingsmill, and Townshend at nomination night, 1937.*

TOP: *Brother John leaving for overseas, April 19, 1941 with Townshend, Ernest and Alvin.*

BOTTOM: *Kathleen and Townshend on their 30th wedding anniversary.*

> tication and by their consequent reliance on the clergy for moral direction. Among Protestants, at least, the generation after the war was different.[4]

Ultimately, if not immediately, the impact of the War and the increasing materialism and secularism of the "roaring twenties" acted as corrosive acids upon the values Canadians had inherited from their Victorian parents and grandparents. The traditional answers the church gave to life's problems began to fade as people turned to other sources for guidance. Yet, for the moment, the churches appeared to retain their central position in Canadian society.

It was a daunting challenge that Townshend faced when he preached his first sermon to his three congregations on August 1, 1926. He chose as his text two verses from Psalm 96.[5] The people of the Church of Ascension, Kingarf, were so moved by their new rector's words that they had a part of his text, "O, worship the Lord in the beauty of holiness", painted around the chancel arch.[6]

Townshend was an immediate "hit" with his flock. It was like being back in Huron County, for the parish of Bervie, Kingarf and Kinlough—which he once described as a miniature diocese—was only a few miles inland from Lake Huron. Its rich soil supported numerous farms scattered along its concession roads. The farmers here were hard-working, God-fearing people. Family, church and school were still important institutions to them. As the statistics of the various denominations show, these farm families still attended church in considerable numbers. While the total number of individuals on Townshend's parish roll did not measurably increase during his rectorship, the average attendance and the financial givings did.[7] One of his former parishioners wrote, "He was a real go-getter and several [families] returned to the church after years of absence. He always liked to feel that the church truly was people marching forward like a mighty army under God's good spiritual guidance."[8]

When Townshend took over, the parish was barely meeting its financial obligations. He set to work to improve this situation immediately. As with so many Anglican congregations at that time, the people had not been trained in the practice of regular giving. There was an endemic spirit of congregationalism in the Diocese of Huron in those years, and parishes rarely looked beyond their own needs when they raised money. Within a year Townshend had persuaded them to increase their contributions. In fact, his parish had the highest percentage of giving in the deanery. He won them over to his own deeply held belief that church people should give not only towards the upkeep of their own local church but also to the wider concerns of the diocese and national church. His approach was a reflection of the episcopal nature of the Anglican Communion and was a theme he constantly pursued during his clerical career.

The Townshends enjoyed their years in Bruce County. As has been pointed out, he had a special rapport with farmers. He talked their language; he understood their problems, their fears, their hopes. "The congregations were chiefly rural folk, and Rev. William [sic], having grown up on a farm, had some knowledge of farmers' problems with machinery. He was always ready and willing to fix or impart any help he could and this was a means of digging into the spiritual roots of the farmer, too. Rev. Wm's [sic] words were, 'I'll see you at church on Sunday', nine times out of ten it worked."[9]

The parish gave Townshend a chance to hone his skills as a pastor and, in responding to this challenge, he quickly earned a reputation as an up-and-coming young cleric. Kathleen and he—for it was very much a team effort—organized a branch of the A.Y.P.A. Using expertise acquired as teachers, they easily attracted the young people, and soon built up the largest and liveliest A.Y. in the deanery. He organized a girls' softball team, which won the local championship two years in a row.[10]

All of this effort was beginning to wear on Kathleen. To their first three children a fourth was added shortly after the move to Bervie in 1926. Looking after this growing brood and the rectory, together with parish activities, became a constant drain on her energy. To alleviate the problem, she asked one of her sisters to move in with them to help.

AFTER THREE HAPPY YEARS in this parish, Townshend in 1929 accepted an appointment to the Church of the Redeemer in London, the see city for Huron. Originally, he had rejected Archbishop Williams' request that he move to the city. Townshend preferred another rural parish near Stratford, one that had offered him a larger stipend and a more commodious house, both of which were more suitable for his growing family. Besides, he was not sure he could handle a city charge. However, he chanced to overhear a senior clergyman commenting that Townshend had made a wise decision since he probably was not suited to be a city rector. This slighting remark stung his pride and provoked him to change his mind. He accepted the London position, much to the amusement and bemusement of the Archbishop.

Townshend's new parish was in the residential area of north-east London. The Church of the Redeemer had grown out of a mission established in 1907 by the larger parish of St. John the Evangelist. By the 1920s a small, undistinguished building had been erected and a rectory added. The congregation still received funding from the diocese. Townshend made it a condition of his accepting the call that the parish must become self-supporting. The vestry readily accepted this challenge even though the members of the congregation were not wealthy. There were only 140 families listed on the parish roll, and the total number of souls, including children, was 460. The average attendance at a Sunday service in 1929 was 100, and the total contributions that year were $2,320.63.[11]

Both priest and parishioners were hopeful of securing their new goal. And why shouldn't they have been? In 1929, optimism about the future was widespread; people were confident that the good times would last forever. Within a few months, however, the world's economy was dealt a devastating blow when the stock market crashed, ushering in the Great Depression. This development hampered the efforts of all denominations to maintain contributions to both local and national efforts.

Little wonder, then, that Townshend found his first year at the Redeemer to be a trying experience. He often wondered if he had not made a serious mistake in accepting this city parish. It was not only the finances; the whole parish seemed a problem. City people were different from their country counterparts. "...they had been accustomed—the people ran the church, not the rector....Everyone wanted his own way. My first year I had to stand up to them on several occasions. I told them

I was going to stay until they learned to like [it] so you'd better start in right away."[12]

Moreover, the family was continuing to grow and Townshend's stipend of 1,400 dollars was not sufficient to cover expenses. So, he turned to his former avocation—dealing in real estate—to augment his salary. He became a shrewd bargainer in this field, and over the years his family, the London School Board, and the Diocese of Huron benefited from his talent. As another cost-saving device he bought a cow and tethered it in a field across from the rectory. Every morning and evening the animal supplied milk for the family's table.

In spite of the difficulties, Townshend soon began to spur his new parish into action. He undertook an extensive programme of home visitations, a scheme that quickly showed results: both the weekly attendance and the offerings grew, with the latter showing an 88 per cent increase over the previous year.[13] At the first vestry meeting of January, 1930, Townshend told his congregation that they "as a church could look on the year just past with gratitude and thankfulness for the progress that had been made in the spiritual and financial conditions of the church."[14] The congregation was delighted with this development and passed a vote of thanks to their rector and his wife "for the excellent work they were doing and had done since they had come to the parish."[15]

The same annual report indicated that the parish had a number of organizations, and Townshend seized on these to further enhance the parish's life. Naturally, the young people received immediate attention. Over the next few years, a vibrant Sunday School was built up, which attracted hundreds of children taught by numerous volunteer teachers who had never been involved in this type of activity until the new rector recruited them. A fresh spirit was injected into the A.Y.P.A., and soon it was involved in a wide range of activities including drama productions, carrying out parish surveys, and building new tennis courts. The latter undertaking, done without the permission of the select vestry, provoked a humorous exchange between two of Townshend's sons. Young John informed Bill that it was really God who had erected the new courts, but Bill, thinking there was something amiss with such a theological explanation, said to John: "I don't believe God had anything to do with it, there wouldn't have been such a big row over it." Townshend himself later admitted, "I've got to confess that his father shared his sentiments."[16]

For the women there was the Altar Guild and the Women's Guild; the latter concentrated on work inside the parish. Kathleen added a branch of the W.A., which the members named in her honour. This group expended its energies on the missionary work of the Church. The men meanwhile had a very active Layman's Association which, among its many projects, repaired and painted the church and rectory.

Perhaps the most spectacular activity undertaken during Townshend's rectorship was the annual spring garden party. This event was eagerly anticipated not only by the congregation but by many of the inhabitants of north London. These parties were happy occasions with attractions for all ages, and lasted for several days. Organizing them was exhausting work, but the rewards, both spiritual and financial, were large. Townshend also held an annual service commemorating the founding of the parish. Engraved invitations listing the guest preachers for the services and the week's events were distributed to all parishioners by the A.Y. Everyone, it seemed, got involved.[17]

Parish picnics were held, first at Port Stanley and later at Springbank Park in London. There were many other events, such as fall bazaars and socials after Sunday's Evensong. These activities created bonds of fellowship among members of the congregation. In a time of serious financial depression, with massive unemployment and social and psychological dislocation, the type of ministry conducted by Townshend was incredibly important. Not only did it build up the material side of the parish, it also enhanced the spiritual lives of many people in those difficult and dreary days. Townshend never forgot that first and foremost he was a pastor, whose primary task was to preach the gospel, to administer the sacraments, and to uplift the penitent, the wayward and the weary.

However, the wider concerns of the diocese and the secular world were offering further challenges. For a man of Townshend's talents and abilities, with strong views on public issues, it was natural that he would attract the notice of his ecclesiastical superiors and of prominent laymen. Very early in his career he was elected to the Executive

Committee of the Synod, which handled all major items of diocesan business between synod meetings. Here his voice began to be heard, and heeded. For a young cleric, this was a notable development.

TOWNSHEND'S FIRST FORAY beyond church duties was in the field of public education. In 1933 two of London's leading educators, H.B. Beal and G.A. Wheable, asked him to run for a seat on the Board of Education in the forthcoming election.[18] At first he demurred, feeling he was not well-known enough in the city. Finally, he agreed; and his two sponsors organized such a skillfully run campaign that he led the poll.[19] He joined his fellow trustees on the board in the new year (1934). He was to occupy this seat almost continuously for 44 years.

Townshend entered upon his new duties as trustee in the same year that the effects of the Depression seriously began to erode school finances across the province.[20] The hard times were making it difficult for trustees to maintain services that had been expanding throughout the 1920s. At the beginning of the thirties, London boasted that it had one of the most complete systems in the province. Along with its numerous elementary and secondary schools, it had a vocational school which had earned an enviable reputation in the field. Also London had pioneered in providing auxiliary classes for the mentally retarded. But the Ontario government's new policy of reducing school grants threatened to undermine this growth, although London's wealth did provide a cushion against the direct impact of the government's action.

Townshend, of course, was well aware of this situation. As the father of many children, he was concerned with the future of the schools. As a cleric who travelled around the city, he saw the devastating effect the Depression was having on families and the career opportunities for young people. As a former teacher he possessed a deep-seated conviction that education could improve a person's chances of having a good life. After all, the public schools had certainly done so for him and two of his brothers. No child, in his opinion, should be denied a similar opportunity, even in the face of current financial stringencies.

At his first board meeting, Townshend immediately injected himself into the debate on these issues by placing a notice of motion before the board asking that a committee be appointed to investigate the possibility of providing free textbooks "to some, or all, pupils in Public School."[21] At first glance this suggestion might seem to be of minor import but, in fact, for many parents with several children attending school, it was a serious matter. While the price of the books was minimal, it was nonetheless a burden for many people. Implementing this policy was one way to alleviate stress on family incomes and, at the same time, to enhance the importance of schooling itself. The board appointed a committee with Townshend as its chairman to investigate the proposal. Based on the committee's recommendations, the board decided to give free textbooks to children taking Geography in Grade 5, Composition and Grammar in Grade 6, English History in Grade 7, and Canadian History in Grade 8. The total cost was estimated to be 1,400 dollars in the first year and 950 dollars in subsequent years. Over the years this practice was broadened to include all subjects in the elementary schools. In the meantime Townshend was gratified with this first attempt, even though it was only a partial victory. He was to become used to limited victories in the political arena.

Pleased with this success, he plunged ahead, bringing other items before the board which he felt needed attention. Two of these became perennial interests for him. The first was the need to improve the salaries, benefits, and working conditions for both teachers and support staff. He persuaded the board to agree that the recent freezing of salaries as a result of the suspension of the government's grant increases for salaries should be regarded as a temporary measure "and if, and when such suspension is lifted, the increased salaries should normally be based on the salary list existing at such time."[22] He also persuaded the board to investigate the possibility of paying pensions to all board employees (other than teachers) when they retired.[23] By the end of his first term, the trustees had adopted a plan to grant these people a retirement allowance. Again this was only a partial solution but, at least, it was the beginning of a better approach until a proper pension plan could be introduced.

His other major area of interest was the high-school curriculum. Townshend was concerned that the academic fare offered in the schools was far too restrictive. This programme, he continuously argued over the coming years, was too limited as it was designed only for adolescents who wanted to attend university, a group that represented only a small proportion of the potential high-school population. Such an education was grossly unfair to a majority of the students, he contended, for most youths needed training to prepare them for immediate employment. He eagerly sought the appointment of a sub-committee to explore the likelihood of increasing the number of courses offered in the city's collegiates.[24] Although a committee was set up to look into this issue, it did not report that year. However, he had begun his campaign for a more liberal high-school programme, and he would harangue trustees in season and out on what he regarded as a vital issue.

Serving on the board brought Townshend to the notice of many prominent public leaders. C.C. Carrothers, a fellow trustee and leading city lawyer, became a lifelong friend even though they often had serious differences at board meetings. Fred Kingsmill, then Mayor of London, a leading Anglican layman and local businessman, and Tom Lawson, another major businessman and scion of an important political family, were just two examples of such men attracted to this able and energetic young cleric. They admired his administrative abilities and the way he spoke for the values and institutions they cherished. These contacts became very useful to Townshend in furthering both his public and clerical careers.

After his successful re-election to the board for 1936,[25] Townshend continued to press for improved salaries for teachers. Better pay not only made life easier for teachers and their families, he argued, but improved their morale. Both students and the population benefited. He was particularly concerned to improve the salaries of newly married teachers. In fact, he wanted to grant them increases as soon as they married. The other trustees balked at this proposal, fearing it would add to their financial burden, especially during the Depression. A compromise was effected which granted newly married men an increase at least equal to the fixed minimum on January 1 of the year following their marriage.[26] Again it was another partial success, but at least some teachers obtained a better wage.

A year later the female secondary teachers asked for salary parity with their male colleagues. Townshend agreed with their arguments and supported their claim. Although nothing was achieved for the moment, here was another issue he vigorously championed in the next few years until the women finally obtained their objective. His efforts to improve their working conditions gained him the support of teachers over the years. He knew what it was like to be a teacher and to raise a family on a small stipend. He had great sympathy for their claims and he consistently supported their efforts.

During his tenure on the board, Townshend served on many committees. In fact, he was appointed or elected to nine in the first term alone. Probably the one which gave him the greatest pleasure—and one on which he served many, many times—was the Vocational Advisory Committee. At that time, and for many years after, this group had virtually total control over all of the academic and financial affairs of the H.B. Beal Technical School. Townshend regarded technical education as being more suitable for most adolescents. To him the practical relevance of the commercial and vocational courses was obvious, especially in the midst of the Depression. In this committee and in his public addresses, he constantly goaded educational officials to improve the image and usefulness of technical education, but it was difficult to persuade others to accept his view. Respect for the collegiate institute was deeply ingrained in the Ontario mind.

In 1935, an old and thorny issue in Ontario education reappeared and spread consternation among public school trustees and supporters across the province. This was the issue of extending more financial assistance to the Roman Catholic Separate Schools. The newly elected Liberal regime of Premier Mitchell Hepburn proposed to give these schools a share of the corporation property tax, a very lucrative source of revenue.[27] The renewal of this battle simply reawakened old animosities. Townshend's position on the problem was unequivocal. As a Protestant, an Orangeman and a member of the Conservative Party, he strenuously denounced the plan. If there was one theme he voiced all during his public career as an educational spokesman, it was a spirited defence of Ontario's public school system. For him the existence of separate schools was an unfortunate aberration. They were divisive both socially and educationally, and it was very wrong, if not injudicious, to encourage their expansion. Such a move struck at the integrity of the public school system and should not be countenanced.

In February, 1935, a deputation of local citizens pleaded with the board to oppose this proposed legislation. The meeting proved to be a very spirited one, and indicated how divisive the government's plan really was. Townshend seized on this event as a springboard from which to launch his attack. He too wanted the board to protest against Hepburn's move, but the trustees split on a motion proposing this kind of direct attack. Another trustee offered a motion requesting the government to appoint a commission to review the problem, but this idea was too tame for Townshend. Conceivably such a commission could give the government a chance to get off the hook. The Roman Catholics might marshall their forces and lobby the commission to grant them some concession, and that kind of a compromise could open the door to all sorts of undesirable possibilities. In spite of his vehement protests, the board accepted the motion. He then succeeded in having a proposal adopted whereby the board would join the local group to interview the premier on this hot topic.[28]

Their effort to dissuade the government failed, and it went on to pass the legislation. However, the defeat of a Liberal candidate in a by-election in the riding of East Hastings prompted Hepburn to take the unusual step of revoking the act in the next session of the Legislature. Apparently he did not want the Separate Schools to become an issue in the forthcoming provincial election slated for sometime in 1937. However, now was not the moment for the public school supporters to drop their guard.[29]

CHURCH DUTIES AND OBLIGATIONS also consumed much of his time even as these exciting educational battles were being fought. In the Synod, Townshend's voice was being heard more often on a wide range of topics, and his opinions were being given careful consideration. Certainly one issue he constantly pushed was the need to improve clergy stipends, especially in the rural areas. Here his arguments were similar to the ones he used at board of education meetings with respect to teachers' salaries. Many clergy families suffered severely in the 1930s. Some priests had not received a full salary for years. Townshend supported a plan, proposed in the Synod of 1934, to create a Stipend Restoration Fund. Part of its funding would come from the diocese's general revenues and the remainder would be contributed by those clergy who felt that they could afford to do so.[30] Yet, even for rectors in the wealthier city parishes, this was a sacrifice. For Townshend, with his large family, it was an even greater one, but he willingly donated to the fund. The establishment of this Fund certainly alleviated the potentially desperate situation of many of the clergy and their families.

In 1936 Townshend was elected to his first major administrative position in the Church. He was chosen as the Rural Dean of East Middlesex. For the next two years he held this post, which gave him oversight of the 16 parishes in the city, together with four others in the surrounding countryside. The position of rural dean is a very ancient one in the Church's hierarchy. The primary function of this official is to make certain that the orders of the bishop and resolutions of synod are carried out. However, the office does not possess extensive authority. The dean must rely upon the ability to persuade and cajole his brother clerics to achieve his purpose. Certainly, Townshend possessed these skills in abundance.

Another function of the rural dean, in those days, was to preside over monthly clergy meetings. Usually these convocations began with a devotional talk, which was followed by an address given by either one of the members or by an outside expert. Often the topic was concerned with a current social issue. The minute book of this deanery for those years indicates that talks were given on a wide variety of subjects. Communism and its relationship to Christianity, other world movements, missions to China, the training of Sunday School teachers, the problem of juvenile delinquency, and the flaws in capitalism were just some of the issues dealt with.[31]

These manifold activities obviously kept Townshend away from his family. Some of them were now adolescents and needed firm guidance during those disturbing years. One way he was able to spend time with them was during the summer. He had been able to persuade the parish to let him have two months free in the summer. Invariably he took his brood to the farm near Bayfield or to the one he had purchased in the Chelsea Green area south of London. It was good to get back to the soil, to return to his roots. These were happy and restful times. It gave him an opportunity to renew his physical and emotional strength and to interact with his children. These holidays partly made up for his increasing absences from home, but at the end of August they all returned to the city, and the interminable round of meetings and activities began again. Each fall seemed to add more responsibilities to his agenda. The younger children saw him less often as the years passed.

At the annual vestry meeting of the parish in January, 1937, Townshend issued a double challenge to his flock. This was the Church's 25th anniversary. Why not try to pay off the mortgage? Moreover, since the present building was becoming too small for the growing congregation, why not start a building fund for a new church? And since the wardens had presented such an excellent financial statement for the preceding year, now was the time to start.[32] No doubt he startled his vestry with these bold plans. After the initial shock the people caught the rector's infectious enthusiasm and took up his challenge. Vestry set a date for the burning of the mortgage. The obvious moment was the annual garden party. A lot of hard work had to be accomplished before then. At the same time, the vestry authorized the rector to look into obtaining preliminary plans for a new building. Amazingly, this congregation, which had limited financial resources, set about to raise money for two major purposes. While most parishes would blanch, Townshend, with his driving energy and vision, boldly drew his congregation into this campaign.

By June sufficient funds had been raised. Parishioners eagerly looked forward to the events which had been planned for this year's garden party. Special services with guest preachers had been arranged, but the highlight of the week was the gala banquet at which Bishop Seager was to be the main speaker. On this evening the mortgage was burned by three people—Mrs. Bessie Geoghan, Mrs. T.J. Ashman and Mr. James McKenzie—who had attended the meeting when an application had first been made to establish the Church of the Redeemer as a separate parish.[33] It was an exhausting but thrilling week. The parish was now debt-free and still growing. Perhaps the time had come to give the rector a full-time assistant curate. This would require more funds, but the congregation was in an ebullient mood. They probably knew that Townshend's name had been mooted as rector of some larger parishes and that he had been recommended as a candidate for an office in the National Church structure.[34] For the moment nothing came of these possibilities, but it was only a matter of time before he would be called to another position.

IN THE MEANTIME THERE was the parish, the growing family, and the business at the London Board of Education. In 1937, Townshend was elected as chairman for the first time. Now he was in a position to advance his favourite projects. In his lengthy inaugural address he examined many of the areas he was anxious for the board to discuss. Teachers' salaries, revising the high-school curiculum, improving school facilities were some of them. Also he began his campaign to have more extensive religious education introduced into the local schools. He wanted the board to adopt the practice which was used in other communities of having the clergy give instruction during regular school hours, not before or after the regularly scheduled classes. He also seized the opportunity to express his support for vocational education, praising the work being done at the Beal Technical School. Townshend warned the board that "Far-sighted employers already foresee, in the near future, a shortage of native Canadian skilled workers."[35] Hence, there was a pressing need to place more emphasis on this type of instruction since the graduates could look forward with confidence to securing employment. The obvious message for the London board was for it to become more deeply involved in vocational education and, at the same time, to begin to revise the traditional high-school curriculum.

With respect to this matter, he heaped praise on a new course called the Cultural Vocational Course, which had been introduced at Sir Adam Beck Collegiate Institute in September, 1936. Townshend wanted this programme, which he described as a combination of academic subjects and "a study of system in the home, the office and the shop, a study of behaviour, deportment and procedure under all circumstances."[36] This course, he argued, should be extended to a three-year-one and placed in all of the local high schools for those students who were not planning to attend university or normal school.

Typically, Townshend laid an extremely busy schedule before his fellow trustees, and he invited them to plunge immediately into his agenda.

At the board's first meeting, they tackled the thorny issue of salaries. The Relations Committee of the local branch of the Ontario Secondary School Teachers' Federation requested the trustees to restore the practice of annual salary increments. Previously, the board had been reluctant to increase its expenditures, but now with the new chairman prodding them on they became more receptive to the teachers' request. Negotiations went rather smoothly, and Townshend was able to report at the end of the year that "The teachers were placed back on their salary schedule and given one-half the automatic increase to which their contracts entitled them."[37] Unfortunately, he had been unable to persuade the board to institute a pension plan for the support staff, but he did keep this issue alive.

Hoping to achieve something substantial for vocational education during his term of office, he appointed a committee composed of the superintendent, the collegiate principals, and representatives from some of the city's service clubs to organize a course on vocational guidance and have it introduced into the high schools.[38] He felt very keenly that young people were not being given adequate guidance about career choices. This lack, he contended, was one of the most serious flaws in the collegiate curriculum. Many service clubs, the Chamber of Commerce, the Provincial Department of Labour, and the University of Western Ontario all sent representatives to meet with this committee as it tried to realize Townshend's goal.[39]

At the same time that this committee was attempting to devise a programme, the Kiwanis Club had organized a very extensive vocational guidance course at Sir Adam Beck Collegiate. It invited speakers to talk to the students about different types of employment, arranged interviews, donated appropriate books to the school's library, and established a scholarship for the students enrolled in the Cultural Vocational Course. Townshend lauded the club's efforts. "The experiment undertaken by the Kiwanians is proving eminently successful, and marks an important advance in the effort to help students to find happy adjustment on leaving school."[40] Now he wanted the other collegiates to have the advantages of a similar programme.

MEANWHILE, AT THE BOARD meeting of September 21, 1937, trustee C.C. Carrothers informed his colleagues that their chairman had been selected as the Conservative Party candidate for the upcoming provincial election.[41] Townshend had been approached by a number of local party officials to allow his name to be put forward at the nomination meeting. He was not certain that entering politics was really something he wanted to do, but then he had always been a very political person. Playing politics, in the best sense of the word, was one of his gifts. He had been a Tory supporter from his youth. His pro-British attitudes and his Orange Lodge background had made him an ardent Conservative supporter. Two items in the current Liberal government's policy had aroused his ire. One, of course, was their scheme to extend more financial assistance to the Roman Catholic Separate Schools and the other was their stand on the public sale of alcoholic liquors.

After carefully discussing the idea with Kathleen and securing the support of his select vestry,[42] he decided to enter the race. The nomination meeting was held on the evening of September 4, 1937 at the Masonic Temple. His only serious rival was his old friend, Fred Kingsmill, the incumbent mayor. The rector easily won the contest. In his acceptance speech he launched a blistering attack on the Hepburn government, which he scornfully labelled "the greatest lawbreakers in the Province of Ontario."[43] Naturally he criticized their separate school legislation and their liquor policy, which would have allowed communities the option of permitting taverns to open. Townshend, who never used spirits, feared this scheme might harm young people, and he bitterly opposed its introduction.

Aware that as a clergyman he would provoke criticism for entering politics, he pointed to the careers of the Rev. Egerton Ryerson, the Methodist minister who had been Superintendent of Education of Ontario from 1846 to 1876 (not a wholly accurate case as Ryerson was an appointed official) and his fellow Anglican cleric, the Rev. Canon Henry Cody, who had been Minister of Education in 1918-1919 during the last days of the Hearst administration. Townshend claimed that he saw no contradiction between serving the church and being involved in politics. He boldly stated, "I look upon this as a call to Christian service," and, he added, "I feel that in serving my fellow men I am serving God."[44]

And so the race was on! It was not an easy contest for the rector. He was pitted against the popular sitting Liberal member, Dr. A.S. Duncan. For a few days the campaign degenerated into a rather nasty affair. Some Liberals began to spread the rumour that the Townshends had had two children before they were married. Dr. Duncan finally stepped in and ordered his supporters to squelch this malicious tale. But in spite of this distasteful episode, Townshend spent a few exciting weeks lambasting the Grits.

His speeches were not simply a negative attack on the government's record. In a large advertisement printed in the *London Free Press* he lent his support to a broad range of social legislation which he claimed the Tories would enact if they were victorious on polling day. He presented himself as a friend of the working man and the unemployed, pledging that he would fight for a wider system of social security, especially contributory schemes for old-age pensions and unemployment insurance. He wanted tax relief for the embattled property owners.[45] He even advocated developing hydro-electric power on the St. Lawrence River system so long as this project did not undercut Canadian labour, "the workingman being Townshend's first consideration"[46] as the advertisement emphasized.

Many of these proposals were traditional nostrums politicians trotted out at election time. Yet, in a very real sense, Townshend's own personal background, his Christian convictions, his experience in pastoring an urban parish during the Depression—all influenced him to support this kind of reform programme. The devastation in people's lives wrought by the recent economic conditions had touched him deeply, and he was determined to use the government to alleviate these sufferings. Government, like the church, was created to serve people and help them have a more abundant life.

However, Townshend's assaults on the Hepburn regime were of little avail, as were those of his leader, Earl Rowe, and many other Tory candidates. The Liberals swept the province. Locally, Dr. Duncan defeated Townshend by 6,200 votes. In spite of his personal popularity, which, no doubt, the Conservatives had counted on, it was a stunning defeat for Townshend.[47] Within a few days of this debacle, though, his natural optimism helped him to readjust to life, as he plunged back into his parish work and activities at the board. There were to be no more forays into provincial politics, but he retained a close connection with the Tory party and its various leaders for the rest of his life.

HARDLY HAD THE EXCITEMENT of the election campaign died down when the Townshend house was enlivened by the birth of their tenth and last child, a son, named Charles Robert. Bob, as he was called, was the only son to follow his father into the Church. Ten children now lived in the rectory; it was becoming crowded. And though he had received some increases in his stipend, he continued to make real-estate deals in order to help make ends meet. Yet these children always had the basic material goods. Any deprivation they may have suffered was compensated for by the love and affection provided by the family. His beloved mother had provided a very loving home for her children; he could do no less reverence to her cherished memory than by emulating her example.

Shortly after Robert's birth on January 18, 1938, his father reported to the annual vestry meeting on the previous year's events, emphasizing that the parish was now free of all financial debt. Surely, this was the moment to move ahead with plans for a new church building. He challenged his flock to raise 42,000 dollars for this project. Vestry, staggered by this astronomical sum, voted to delay making a decision for the moment. Even though he kept exerting pressure on his people to start a campaign, he was unsuccessful in achieving anything before he left the parish for another appointment.

It was the Diocese of Huron's need for a skilled administrator which drew him out of the parochial work. By the late 1930s the diocese's finances were in perilous shape. The Depression had prevented many parishes from contributing to the diocesan coffers. Bishop Seager had not proved to be a very skillful administrator. The diocese needed someone who could inject vitality into its administrative structure and, at the same time, persuade the congregations to adopt more effective techniques of financial planning. The Synod appointed a search committee to seek someone who could undertake this important work.

After reviewing several names, the committee recommended Townshend to the Bishop, who immediately accepted their report[48] and offered him the post. Obviously, if he accepted, it meant resigning as rector. The parish, quite naturally unhappy about the offer, agreed to grant him a sabbatical leave, but the Bishop summarily rejected this proposal.[49] Townshend was needed immediately. On January 23, 1939 he submitted his final report to the vestry of the Church of the Redeemer.[50] Shortly afterwards he and his family moved out of the rectory. His acceptance of the new appointment effectively ended his tenure as a parish priest. He now held the office of Diocesan Commissioner and, at the same time, the Bishop appointed him a Canon of St. Paul's Cathedral.[51] Townshend had made a significant move in his clerical career.

CHAPTER THREE

The Diocesan Commissioner

On February 1, 1939, Townshend officially assumed his new post as Commissioner for the Diocese of Huron. This diocese had always been one of the largest in the Canadian Church, both in area and in numbers of parishes. Territorially it covered most of south-west Ontario, stretching from Brantford at its eastern end to Windsor in the west and from Lake Erie on the south to Tobermory on the northern tip of the Bruce Peninsula. This was an incredibly large district to administer and had always taxed the energies of its bishops. In 1939 much of its economy was still based on farming and farm-related industries. Dotted throughout the area were a number of cities and towns, such as Windsor, Brantford, St. Thomas, Paris, Kitchener, Waterloo, and Galt—all of which had factories and plants. London, the see city, was the home of many financial organizations and possessed the diocese's only major institution of higher learning, the University of Western Ontario, founded in 1878.

At the time of Townshend's appointment the diocese had 140 priests serving 150 parishes but, since many of the rural ones often had more than one congregation within their borders, there were really 267 congregations with 88,852 Anglicans listed on their rolls.[1] The parishes were grouped into 14 rural deaneries and four archdeaconries. The Bishop, the Rt. Rev. Charles Seager, who had assumed this office in 1932, was, of course, the chief administrator of the diocese. All of the clergy were responsible to him and, as his voluminous correspondence indicates, he was deeply involved in every aspect of their lives. In an episcopal church, the bishop is not simply a business manager; he is also the chief sacramental official of the diocese and the father-in-God to all of his people, both clerical and lay. It is to him the clergy turn for advice and help on a wide range of problems, parochial and personal. Thus, in any diocese, the bishop carries a heavy burden, to which is added duties as a member of the house of bishops of both the provincial and general synods and involvement in the work of the world-wide Anglican communion.

As has been previously stated, the finances of the diocese had reached their nadir by the end of the 1930s. Townshend was appointed to breathe new life into the diocese's financial structure. The selection committee had given him only very general guidelines relating to his duties as Diocesan Commissioner.[2] Townshend was therefore free to set the parameters of the position himself, and he lost no time in doing so. He quickly immersed himself in the variegated details of the diocese's life. He undertook an immediate survey of the finances, and was somewhat dismayed by what he discovered. At the same time, he also became a trouble shooter for Bishop Seager, who asked Townshend to investigate problems within various parishes.

Shortly after he assumed office, Townshend began dashing around south-west Ontario dealing with the minutiae of local issues and disputes. He travelled to the parish of Bayfield, where he had grown up, to persuade the congregation to install an indoor toilet in the new rectory. And this was in 1939! On another occasion he helped the parish of Mitchell recover from a disastrous fire that had completely destroyed their church. Later in the year he mediated a disagreement between two disputing congregations in the parish of Norwich and Oxford.[3] Day after day he was on the road mending fences, binding up wounds, resolving disputes. Invariably his reports to the Bishop indicated that a happy solution had been effected. Townshend, as we have seen, possessed an innate optimism, and he may have sugar-coated some of his comments in his reports. Congregations can be intractable and difficult, and often need to be cajoled or coerced into accepting a solution. Such activities forced him to use his diplomatic and managerial skills to the utmost but, at the same time, it brought him into touch with every facet of the diocese's work. He enjoyed it thoroughly.

A pattern of work soon established itself. For the next several years he toured the diocese, speaking to deanery meetings about budgets, preaching in numerous churches (on two occasions he preached five times in one day), interviewing wardens and parochial committees, and always pleading the Church's cause. In his first two years he travelled 66,000 miles.[4] These activities created a sense of loyalty and affection towards Townshend, which he was able to invoke in support of many causes in later years.

Soon the Bishop, the archdeacons and congregations were constantly seeking his advice. By November, 1939, Bishop Seager had to tell the church wardens in Florence who were searching for a new rector that, "I find the Diocesan Commissioner, Canon Townshend, is so very over-loaded with work already that it is impossible for him to take the matter up personally at the present."[5] Everyone, it seemed, wanted his expertise.

Yet it was the diocese's finances that really had first call on his attention. The diocese had not been able to meet its National Church apportionment, and the Bishop thought this was reprehensible for a diocese of this size. Clearly, a carefully designed fund-raising campaign was needed. Huron had not had one in many years. The immediate purpose, obviously, was to raise a sufficiently large sum of money to offset the current crisis. But, at the same time, a larger objective loomed, that of teaching church people to donate in a more systematic manner.

In May, 1939, Synod decided to launch a campaign to raise 20,000 dollars. This was a tremendous undertaking at such a moment in time. A major effort was needed to overcome the lethargy of the congregations and their ingrown attitude of congregationalism. Townshend faced an exciting challenge. Ever resourceful, he utilized a variety of old but successful fund-raising techniques. From the outset he was determined to have wide participation by the laity. Every deanery was required to set up committees to co-ordinate the canvass in all of its parishes, while each parish had to organize a visit to all of its members. The burden of this latter enterprise fell on the shoulders of the laity. Townshend had pamphlets prepared explaining the diocese's needs, and distributed them to all Church people. Bishops from other dioceses were recruited as speakers. By the end of the year his efforts, in spite of the continuing Depression and the beginning of the Second World War, had been remarkably successful. His supervisory committee were delighted that he had been able to accomplish so much in a short period of time. But not all of the credit belonged to him. The parish clergy led and galvanized their people into action. No doubt the campaign literature had opened the eyes of many churchgoers who had previously contributed simply out of habit. They had never really known about the Church's needs. For many this was the first time they had really encountered any description of the Church's work on both the diocesan and national level. The success of this campaign laid a solid base for future developments, and Townshend was quick to seize the opportunity to build on it.

TOWNSHEND'S INTENSE involvement in his new ecclesiastical duties did not detract from his responsibilities at the Board of Education. At a special meeting in late August, 1939, a few days before the War began, he supported a decision to implement a comprehensive course for the high schools called Mental and Physical Hygiene. The board had asked its medical officer, Dr. John Wilkey, to prepare an outline for this course. In his covering letter to Superintendent G.A. Wheable, Wilkey argued that, "It is desirable that emphasis be given to the promotion of Good Health [sic] as a valuable component of good citizenship and that the course be not merely a study of elementary anatomy and physiology."[6] Townshend enthusiastically endorsed this proposal. It made schooling practical and relevant to adolescents' needs. It helped them to prepare for life, not just for more academic study.

With the outbreak of the War a few weeks later, the trustees were immersed in a completely new set of problems. Supplying the cadets with uniforms, leasing one of its buildings to the local military district, and responding to requests from male teachers for leave to enter the armed services were just a few of the War-related demands. Townshend moved a resolution which guaranteed that teachers would not lose their seniority if they enlisted, and that their pension and group-insurance contributions would be assumed by the board.[7]

With the end of the so-called "phony war" in the spring of 1940, as the Nazi hordes swept through the Low Countries and then France, Canadians of all ages began to assume obligations they had never previously considered. Children and adolescents were mobilized to defend Western civilization against the Fascist onslaught. As R.M. Stamp has written, "The Second World War affected the daily routine of the schools in a myriad of ways....The normal pattern of high school attendance was severely disrupted, with early spring closures and late fall openings the norm throughout most of the province in order to release teenage labour for farm work."[8] London's schools, of course, were affected in similar ways. Townshend represented the board at a meeting with officials of the provincial government and the Urban Trustees Association in August, 1940, which discussed ways of releasing boys from school to work on farms. He reported that the trustees had "promised their co-operation in the enrolment of boys as farm helpers and of secondary school girls in the prosecution of the sale of War Saving Certificates."[9] Based on this decision he asked his fellow trustees to delay opening London's schools until the middle of September, but they rejected his proposal and carried on as usual. They did not think that many boys from urban areas would volunteer for farm work.[10]

EVEN THOUGH THE WESTERN world was rocked by the lightning thrust of the German army in May, 1940, the diocesan Synod, meeting in that month, had a reason for rejoicing. The target for the special appeal had been oversubscribed by almost 2000 dollars, and the incredible sum of $95,157.55 had been raised for the diocesan budget. This was almost 30,000 dollars more than had been contributed during the previous year.[11] The Church had used its own style of blitz to improve its condition.

Naturally, Bishop Seager attributed much of this success to Townshend's leadership. And, of course, this was accurate. Indeed, by the end of 1940 Townshend had persuaded one-half of the parishes to adopt the scheme of submitting payments towards the diocesan budget on a regular basis. Previously, most parish treasurers had waited until the end of the year before they submitted their donations. This practice made it difficult for diocesan officials to meet their obligations or to make long-term plans. Under this new system, the diocese had a more adequate cash flow, permitting it to pay its bills, especially its contributions to the work of the General Synod.

Now that Townshend had the congregations moving in what he considered to be the proper direction, how could the momentum be continued? He proposed to the newly created diocesan budget committee, of which he was the chairman, the possibility of introducing the Every Member Canvass (E.M.C.). Under this programme each parish would conduct an annual canvass of its members, asking them to direct their time and talents towards the Church's work. Raising funds, however, was not the sole purpose of this approach; there was a spiritual dimension to the scheme. The essence of it was to teach sacrificial stewardship. Synod readily endorsed his suggestion and decided that the canvass should be carried out in the fall months.[12] Townshend himself anticipated that the scheme would be very helpful in increasing givings to diocesan needs, but only time would tell how readily people would respond to it.

Apart from his efforts to improve the finances, he was still assisting the Bishop in trying to solve congregational problems. For example, the parish of Florence asked for his assistance in seeking a proper site for its new rectory, and the Rev. M.H. Elston sought his assistance in getting the people of Huntingford and Zorra to pay his stipend.[13] While most of these disputes were settled amicably, they did consume much of his time.

Townshend's financial abilities were receiving recognition from the National Church. The Primate of the Church of England in Canada, the Most Rev. Derwyn Owen, appointed him to the executive committee of the Missionary Society of the Canadian Church (M.S.C.C.) in 1940 and, at the same time, placed him on the General Synod's Apportionment Committee together with this committee's major subgroup. As Townshend told the Huron Synod, "Membership on these committees has been most helpful to me as I learn more and more of the task of the Canadian Church."[14] Thus he was launched into the centre of the National Church's financial and administrative affairs. Moreover, these assignments brought him into close contact with episcopal leadership across the country. For the next quarter of a century he served on these committees, and other national bodies, and earned a reputation as a man who had a clear understanding of the intricacies of the Church's financial affairs and who was an efficient and skillful chairman of many of these groups.

Certainly the Church's business was never very far from Townshend's mind. But then, so too were his family's activities. The oldest child, John, was now 20, while Robert, at three, was still a growing infant. Many people were amazed at the size of the household. Indeed, it often became the target of many humorous comments. One night he was driving one of the boys home from a baseball game held on the grounds of St. Peter's Roman Catholic Seminary in London. As father and son drove down the street, they chanced to meet three boys who belonged to the Roman faith cycling in the opposite direction. Seeing the clerical collar, the first two lads said, "Good evening, Father," but the third boy, who was much more knowledgeable about these things scornfully informed his chums, "He's no Father. He has ten kids."[15]

In 1941 tragedy struck the family twice. Kathleen and he were involved in a serious car accident in downtown London. He received a broken shoulder, but was not invalided, while Kathleen suffered extensive injuries and had to convalesce for a time.[16] Then later in the year he received the news that his brother, John, who had joined the Canadian army as an officer, had been drowned when the troop ship on which he was travelling to England had been torpedoed by a German submarine off the coast of Ireland. John's death was a severe blow to Townshend, for this was the second of his siblings to have died at an early age.

Still, life went on and he continued with his challenging work at both the church and the board. In the midst of his grief he reiterated his deepest belief that "We know that nothing is impossible for God with man's co-operation. If we most faithfully do our part, God will in a most abundant measure give the increase."[17] For Townshend the building of the Kingdom of God was a joint venture: God needed man's willing assistance. Townshend's doctrine included a high regard for man, whom he did not view as a totally depraved creature. And while sin was a real aspect of this earthly life and had to be eradicated or at least controlled, this was still God's world, and with a genuine effort, man and God working together could improve it and make it more habitable.

Here then was the reason for trying to get more laymen involved in the Church, not simply as nominally baptised members but as willing helpers who would give their time and talents to God's work. Often, when he was pushing and advising recalcitrant rural deans, rectors, wardens and congregations, it must have been difficult for him to keep this attitude alive; but it was his constant lodestar.

INSTITUTIONS WERE OFTEN just as difficult to deal with as individuals. Huron College's financial affairs were a constant nagging item on Townshend's crowded agenda. As a member of the college's council, he was constantly faced with this issue. When he rejoined the council in 1939 (he would remain a member until 1966), he discovered that the college had a large debt which, despite the use of various expedients, continued to grow. By 1941, when old Principal Waller retired, the debt had mushroomed to the astronomical sum of 17,000 dollars. The new principal, the Rev. Henry O'Neil, a vigorous and energetic man, immediately set about to reduce this sum and, at the same time, to try to enhance the institution's reputation.

Beginning in 1941, Townshend became a member of the college's Finance Committee and its Maintenance and Purchasing Committee. The latter one was responsible for securing the daily necessities. Right away he introduced measures to reduce the cost of procuring food supplies by "buying at a minimum."[18] He negotiated contracts with Parnell's Bakery to buy bread at six-and-a-quarter cents a loaf and with Gold Seal Dairies to pay ten cents for a quart of milk. These economies were designed to check the overspending in the annual budget, which had become a perennial problem at the college.

Yet even these expedients were not sufficient to stem the outflow of money. The mortgage was still hanging over the council's head, and paying the interest on it was becoming ever more difficult. In June, 1942, Bishop Seager pressed the council to try to retire it as quickly as possible and, at the same time, to secure sufficient funds to offset the annual deficit, which was still accumulating. The Bishop feared that a period of financial confusion might develop after the ending of the War, similar to what had ocurred after the First World War, and that it would be detrimental to the college's financial state.[19]

The council appointed a special financial committee, on which Townshend served, to seek a permanent solution to these problems. However, despite their labours no remedy seemed in sight. Then suddenly the Bishop hit upon a unique idea. The federal government had imposed an excess profits tax on businesses during the War, but had allowed companies to reduce this levy by contributing to various designated charities. Why not try to tap this potentially lucrative source? Funds for a new building might even be secured. The Bishop met with several local businessmen to sound them out on this possibility. Based on their response, another campaign committee was struck, with E.A. Wilson as its chairman.[20] Wilson's efforts rapidly produced results. Within five months he had obtained pledges from several companies, and by the end of September, 1943, over 100,000 dollars had been pledged.[21] At the December meeting of the council, a Building Committee was appointed to secure plans for a new structure.[22] Townshend, not unnaturally, was a member of this group. The idea was to sell the old property and move the college up to Western Road near the university. However, disposing of the St. James Street lot and erecting a new college did not occur for a number of years. Nonetheless, these efforts, undertaken in the midst of the War, lifted the institution out of its lethargic state and gave it an injection of vitality and hope for better days ahead.

WHILE THE COLLEGE'S finances verged on the intractable, those of the diocese were looking much sounder. By the middle of 1941, it was obvious that Townshend's efforts to rebuild them had been successful. The upswing in the economy, owing to the War, combined with the introduction of the various techniques to improve giving in the diocese, had contributed to the improved situation. Now it was time for another major improvement. He persuaded Synod to adopt a "pay as you go policy", similar to the one he had the Board of Education adopt years earlier. He told Synod in 1941 that this scheme was "the only way to become relieved of that maddening drive for funds at the end of the year."[23] He devised a three-prong scheme to assist parishes and deaneries to meet their obligations. First, he wanted the parochial Boards of Management (as the select vestries were now to be called) to meet monthly and review their financial situation. Specifically, they were to ensure that the parish's diocesan apportionment was being met and that the parish was paying its bills. Secondly, he wanted the deanery chapters to become more actively involved in the finances by reviewing the state of each parish's givings and offering assistance to any congregation that was falling behind. Lastly, he asked for the creation of a Diocesan Committee on the State of the Church to oversee this work. Synod, now conversant with Townshend's methods, readily agreed.[24] Townshend was quickly becoming the czar of Huron's finances, and his power was becoming very wide and sweeping. However, he was careful to maintain good relations with the parish clergy. For example, he refrained from lashing Synod with harsh comments about the endemic congregationalism of the diocese. This role was left to the Bishop, who rarely let a Synod meeting pass without attacking this attitude. Townshend's efforts, in fact, were gradually undermining this spirit.

The machinery for improving finances was now in place, but getting people to respond was a different matter. His report to Synod on the E.M.C. showed that success was still confined to urban centres. The farming communities lagged behind. The committee wanted more rural members placed on it so that a different policy for E.M.C. in the countryside could be devised.[25] There were also parishes in the cities which had not conducted a canvass that year, and so Synod requested that all parishes do so in the coming fall. One way or another, Townshend was determined to make Huron a solvent diocese.

Yet, not all the clergy eagerly accepted his directives. One rector, who had carried out a very effective canvass in his own parish, complained to Seager that too much emphasis was being placed on the financial aspects of E.M.C. to the detriment of the spiritual side. He noted that many of the clergy had become pessimistic about the work of the Church. He suggested holding an evangelistic campaign to renew their flagging spirits.[26] Some of the clergy, it appeared, were becoming restive, perhaps even resentful, of Townshend's importunings.

IT WAS NOT JUST IN the Church that Townshend ran afoul of the rural communities; he did so as a member of the Senate of the University of Western Ontario. For decades the rural population had been declining, but during the War the exodus from the countryside became more pronounced. For reasons which are not very clear, the senate became exercised about this issue, and created a Committee on Co-operation with Agriculture to try to ascertain the reasons for this decline. Townshend, with his extensive knowledge of rural affairs, was made a member.[27] At the initial meeting he vigorously stated that, in his opinion, the reasons lay in the fact that the "social position of the farmer and agricultural worker has been so cried down that everybody with a modicum of brains left farming to those who don't do anything else."[28] He pleaded with the committee to try to improve the farmer's status, and to enlist the aid of school and church in this endeavour.

During the next year the committee deliberated. It had the university's Economics Department prepare a report on the situation. The findings indicated that, owing to various technological factors, the size of the average farm in the area had been increasing since about 1900, and that this trend would undoubtedly continue into the future. As a means of improving the farmer's financial situation, the report recommended limiting the amount of production in order to drive up the price of farm goods. Townshend feared this approach would touch off a round of inflation, and thus undercut any advantages to the farmer. The committee continued to debate the issue, but, in the end, it failed to offer any specific proposals. After a time there were no references to it in the senate's minutes. Either it was disbanded or it simply stopped meeting.

AS READERS OF THE *London Free Press* unfolded their papers on the evening of January 10, 1941, their eyes met this screaming headline: "Study Revamping of C.I. Curriculum: Courses Unsuitable, Many Wasting Time, School Board Told."[29] C.C. Carrothers had launched a blistering attack on the high-school programme, and was readily supported by Townshend. Together they persuaded the board "to investigate the desirability of revising the Secondary School curriculum to provide a more general type of education; and further to investigate the proposal that a school for the education of girl students be opened offering to high school entrants courses in home economics, household administration, clothing, foods and nutrition, physical and mental hygiene, home nursing and allied courses."[30] Their motion also authorized the board to negotiate with the Department of Education about the introduction of this scheme once the board had devised a definite course.

After carrying out an intensive review, the appointed committee submitted in October a detailed report, which contained a series of recommendations calling for a sweeping revision of the high-school programme. A new certificate programme to help students get ready to enter the workplace was needed immediately, the report argued. This programme should be substantially different from the current university-oriented one. The committee also requested the board's permission to ask the University of Western Ontario if it would accept this certificate as an acceptable entrance requirement for the Home Economics Course (at Brescia Hall) and the Business Administration programme.[31]

A month later the board instructed Superintendent G.A. Wheable and the collegiate principals to begin organizing one group of students in each of the local high schools to take this course. In addition to discussing the acceptability of the new course with the university, the trustees decided to ask the two hospitals, Victoria and St. Joseph's, if they would accept this certificate as a proper entrance requirement for their nursing schools.[32] In September, 1942, the course was started at the Grade 10 level, and the board was told that 50 per cent of the students had opted to take it.[33]

The wheels had been set in motion. A successful assault against the academic bastion had been made. But would it last? Academics, deeply entrenched in the Ontario school system, could use their position to derail these proposals. For the moment, Townshend and his allies were pleased at the prospects. Such reforms might persuade more adolescents to remain in school. Undoubtedly, this was another reason for the support he gave that same year to the idea of extending vocational guidance throughout the entire London school system. This idea was fostered by the Vocational Guidance Committee, who wanted the schools to take a more active role in helping youngsters make decisions about their life careers. Townshend, long an advocate of this role for the schools, eagerly lent his aid to the cause.

It was these issues, together with several others, which highlighted the inaugural speech for his second term as chairman of the board. At the outset, he argued that the board must implement this new programme immediately, "...if we are to help boys and girls of today to meet the problems which will confront them at the close of the war."[34] This statement was made just a month after the Japanese attack on Pearl Harbour, and with the Axis powers still gaining victories everywhere and seemingly invincible. Only Townshend's brand of optimism was strong enough to utter such comments then. He informed the board that the universities had shown interest in the new course but had not yet decided if it was sufficient for university entrance.[35]

He then turned his attention to another aspect of the secondary school which he found deplorable. This was the time and attention devoted to preparing students to write examinations. This "grad grind" approach detracted from the true purposes of education, which he defined as "the desirability of developing in their students personality and initiative and those desirable traits of character such as integrity, dependence, and industry."[36] Finally, he noted with enthusiasm the introduction of religious education into all of the Grade 7 classes in London. Now he wanted this subject extended to all grades.

The importance of the speech lay more in its general principles than in its specific details. It summarized Townshend's educational ideas at this point in time. For him, schooling was more than simply instruction in the three *R's*, important though they were. Significant values had to be transmitted to young people, values that were rooted in Christianity, and were at the heart of Western civilization, for which a major war was currently being waged. Knowledge, morality, and vocational guidance were all linked in an effort to help develop the whole child as he or she was introduced to the more abundant life. To train only the brain was a serious dereliction of the school's duty. These attitudes became the cornerstone of his efforts to reform and improve the public school system.

However, as exciting as curriculum revision and these other matters might be to the members of the board, the events and pressures of the War continued to intrude upon their tasks. The shortages in materials made it difficult to carry out needed repairs to buildings and, of course, it was impossible to erect new ones. Teachers and office staff began to seek cost of living bonuses to offset rising prices. The board tried to grant these allowances, but its financial resources were limited. Even Townshend, who usually supported this kind of request, voted against granting them, as he did for giving bonuses to those who had earned degrees.[37]

The War also had an impact, sometimes quite drastic, on students' lives. Many boys, given leave to work on farms and in war industries, were distracted from spending time on their studies. Sir Adam Beck Collegiate took the unprecedented step of abolishing all tests and examinations for the remainder of the conflict, "in the hope of relieving to some extent the additional strain imposed upon students by existing world conditions."[38]

The War also had a deleterious effect on some children, especially the younger ones. There was a notable increase in juvenile delinquency. Much of this situation was attributed to the lack of supervision at home. With so many fathers away on active service and many mothers working, children were not receiving the usual kind of guidance. The London board tried to offset this development by opening its schools between 7 a.m. and 6 p.m. During the off-school hours, supervision and recreation was provided for the children. The unexpected emergence of this problem provoked Townshend to push harder for more religious instruction as a means of keeping youngsters away from criminal activity.

In fact, a widespread demand for more religious education had recently become something of a crusade across the province. Many other centres had adopted schemes similar to London's. Spokesmen linked Christianity with the preservation of democracy. Hence, it was natural to depict the War as an attempt to preserve Western civilization against the godless Fascist powers. In Ontario there was no more outspoken champion of religious education than George Drew, the leader of the Ontario Conservative Party and a friend of Townshend.

In the provincial election of 1943, Drew made religious education one of his most prominent promises. And while the Tories formed only a minority government, Drew, undaunted, plunged ahead with his proposals. By 1944 a new system of teaching religion in Ontario's schools was introduced. Basically this scheme permitted the clergy to have two one-half-hour slots in the timetables of the elementary schools each week to instruct children in religious studies. Townshend, quite naturally, heartily endorsed this plan.[39]

AS THE WAR ADVANCED towards its close, governments and organizations began to lay plans for the post-war world. Reconstruction and rehabilitation became the watchwords of the day. The British government issued the famous Beveridge Report, which became the basis of that country's welfare state. Many English Anglican authorities welcomed the scheme. They saw it as a logical extension of the gospel and as a reflection of the social philosophy of the recently deceased Archbishop of Canterbury, the dynamic and prophetic William Temple. In Canada the administration of W.L. Mackenzie King produced a similar document, the Marsh Report, but Ottawa did not implement many of its recommendations. Unlike their English counterparts, Canadian Anglican leaders were very cautious about espousing the idea of a welfare state.[40]

Townshend became deeply involved in plans for post-war reconstruction in both education and the church. In December, 1943 he persuaded the board to establish a Post-War Planning Committee whose role was "to survey all the possible post-war needs of our Educational System with a view to expansion."[41] That last word became more prominent than anyone could possibly have envisaged in 1943. Within the Church there were calls for reorganization and expansion also, even in the midst of the War. In 1943, the General Synod established a programme for renewal that included revision of the Prayer Book (a perennial Anglican topic), the opening of possible union discussions with other denominations, and the launching of a major financial campaign to be called the Anglican Advance Appeal.[42] Townshend was to become a major leader in that campaign.

On the diocesan level a Forward Commission was created, largely as a result of pressure from laymen. Its task was "to study ways and means of strengthening the work of the Church and to formulate plans for the raising of the necessary funds."[43] The Executive Committee endorsed this plan and made Townshend its chairman.[44] So, to his already onerous duties as Diocesan Commissioner were added this new and vital task, and one that had to be pursued as quickly as possible.

The Diocesan Synod met a few days after the German surrender in May, 1945. It was very appropriate that amid the rejoicing this body should receive a lengthy and detailed report from its Forward Commission. Hoping to capitalize on the extensive support the Church had developed during the War, the report argued that "effective methods must be adopted to bring the work of the Church home to every member than has been done in the past. It believes that as knowledge of this work is disseminated a revived interest will stimulate church attendance; and this increased church attendance will in turn be the means of a great spiritual stimulation."[45]

A number of suggestions were then explored as ways of achieving this goal. A church bulletin or newspaper was needed to inform the laity of the Church's activities and of future plans. Such a journal could keep people more closely in touch with projects being undertaken in various parishes. Hopefully such an enterprise would create a deeper spirit of unity in the diocese. The younger generation, the obvious source of supply for the Church's future leaders, needed more attention, the report declared. Hence, the building of a church camp was proposed. Now that the public schools had included religious studies in the curriculum, the Church had an opportunity to redesign its Sunday School programme. Moreover, Sunday Schools should also copy the new practice of the secular schools in using audio-visual equipment. The Church had to keep pace with society at large.

The report's authors realized that there was going to be some population growth, especially in the urban centres. This, of course, would ultimately mean constructing new churches and facilities. Therefore, the diocese should be prepared to assist people with both financial and moral support as they tried to make their new congregations self-sufficient. Because much of the leadership for this building programme would fall on the shoulders of the clergy, the report emphasized the need to recruit "active men physically as well as spiritually equipped."[46] Therefore, the existing pension scheme needed to be extensively revised so that older clergy, who had carried the burden during the Depression and the War, could retire at age 65 with a decent remuneration. Finally, the commission recommended setting up subcommittees in each deanery to promote the acceptance of the Commission's proposals.

The report set out an extremely ambitious and comprehensive scheme but, given Townshend's success in advocating and implementing similar measures in the past, it presented a reasonably realistic set of goals. It certainly reflected his basic belief that if people are sufficiently educated about the Church's needs, they will gladly respond. The expectations which people had for a better world in 1945 could easily be channelled into support for these schemes.

Synod enthusiastically endorsed the report and gave its blessing for a financial campaign to raise 50,000 dollars to pay for three immediate needs which the commission argued were most urgent; that is, the creation of a bulletin, the building of a church camp, and the acquisition of new offices for the diocesan officials.[47] The timing of the campaign was crucial since the National Church was also planning to conduct one, and it would be unwise to duplicate efforts. The executive committee was to pick the date for the beginning of the Huron campaign. Synod members went home with their heads buzzing with schemes for expansion and growth. Now they had to inject the same spirit of enthusiasm into their fellow parishioners.

While he was trying to settle these diocesan and educational affairs, his own family needed attention. Ten children were a terrific drain on his financial resources, especially since the older ones were now moving into their own careers and the teenagers found themselves living in a very different world, and needed much guidance and emotional support. Kathleen and he were delighted that John, Bill, Eleanor and Betty had all decided to become teachers. Life was often difficult for the younger ones. Father travelled a good deal, leaving much of the upbringing to Mother. Struggling with ten different personalities, looking after the house, and seeing that bills were paid placed a heavy burden on Kathleen. And bills for rent, clothing and food *had* to be paid. By 1944, the family's finances were in such dire straights that Townshend asked the executive committee for an increase in his stipend. Specifically, he requested and received a rent subsidy and travel allowance. For the moment, these additions eased the burden.[48]

After General Synod announced that *its* financial campaign would begin in the spring of 1946, the diocesan executive committee, attempting to steal a march on the national effort, decided to hold its canvass in November, 1945. Townshend was given general oversight, and empowered to hire an assistant.[49] Using all his familiar techniques for fund-raising and bombarding the laity with informative literature, Townshend raised just over one-half of the targeted amount by the end of December, and by the time he submitted a report to Synod in April, 1946, 60 per cent had been achieved.[50] Diocesan officials did not wait for the campaign to be completed before they started to use the funds for the three designated purposes. A building next to the cathedral was obtained for offices, a property was secured near Bayfield for a church camp, and three issues of the new *Huron Church News* were published.[51] It was a magnificent effort in such a short span of time, and much of the success was owing to Townshend's organizational abilities although, as always, he gave due praise to the numerous clergy and laymen who had worked so hard to obtain these results. Certainly the efforts of these few months had laid a solid foundation upon which the diocese could build its post-war edifice.

Archbishop Seager (as he had become in 1944) sought a way to reward Townshend for his past efforts. What could he do for Townshend? He already held a canon's stall in the cathedral. The next rank in the hierarchy was the position of archdeacon, but in the Anglican Church that post was usually held by an incumbent parish priest. Townshend, of course, had not held a parish since 1939. After consulting with the diocesan chancellor, E.R. Wigle, and the four archdeacons, the Bishop decided to create a new archdeaconry to be called the Archdeacon of Huron, encompassing the entire diocese. Townshend was to have this dignity. In announcing his decision to the new archdeacon, Seager told him that, "The creation of the Archdeaconry of Huron, therefore, without any local jurisdiction, will establish a relationship between you and all the clergy of the Diocese [sic] which we are sure will be of assistance to you in your work as Commissioner."[52] Townshend was pleased that his work had been rewarded in this manner. In his reply to Seager, thanking him for the honour, Townshend let slip that being Diocesan Commissioner was a "somewhat difficult task", and he felt that "this new position and dignity would be of real assistance to me in my work as Commissioner."[53]

A SIMILAR SPIRIT OF enthusiasm for renewal was evident at the board. The new chairman for 1945, F.C. McAlister, warned the trustees that 1945 would probably be a pivotal year in history.[54] He immediately appointed two new committees to handle certain pressing issues facing the board. One of these, of which Townshend was a member, was designated the Relations Committee. Its task was to secure a corps of highly qualified teachers for the city and to seek ways of improving the teachers' salaries, benefits and working conditions. Also, this group was charged with keeping the public informed about the complex problems facing their expanding system of schools.

Townshend was made chairman of the other new committee. This one was charged with designing a revised curriculum for the secondary level. McAlister anticipated that London's recent experiments in the high-school programme would be integrated into the committee's recommendations. Moreover, he hoped that their suggestions would be helpful to the recently appointed Royal Commission on Education, of which Townshend was also a member.[55] His presence on both of these committees produced some startling results within the next year.

The curriculum committee held several meetings, but instead of developing another high-school programme it decided to prepare a brief for the Royal Commission. A unique approach to developing this document was adopted. Committees of teachers from each subject area were appointed to draw up recommendations for each of their particular disciplines. The board committee then compiled these reports and used them as the basis for its own brief. Hence, for the first time, teachers were included in an exercise of policy making. The resulting document, which will be discussed later, proposed some striking and innovative reforms for the secondary programme.

Expansion, both of the city itself and the school system, occupied much of the board's agenda that year and for the next two succeeding decades. London's population had grown during the War, and it was about to take another leap forward. Coupled with the population explosion was a physical expansion of the city. As with so many cities across North America, London started to accumulate suburbs, where new young families began to reside and where they started to produce hordes of children. Within a few years, the "baby boom" generation would be knocking on the schoolhouse doors.

Even in 1945 London had a shortage of facilities. The board recognized this predicament and began to acquire property for future school sites. In fact, the board had a Vacant Property Committee for some time, on which Townshend served. His knowledge of real estate and his expertise in obtaining property made him a valuable member, and he soon began to make advantageous deals for the school system (just as he did for the Church). But all this lay in the future—the post-war era.

CHAPTER FOUR

The Crowded Years

Expansion quickly became one of the primary features of post-war society, and for Canadians it was coupled with an unprecedented period of economic prosperity that lasted for almost three decades. The returning troops found employment in new peace-time industries, bought homes in the newly emerging suburbs, and began to raise families. Gone were the grey, weary days of the Depression and the War. Although still haunted by the despair and sadness of both cataclysmic events, Canadians were determined to build a better world, one that would offer a large measure of security against the type of deprivations which people had endured over the previous 15 years. Both the churches and the schools were expected to play a central role in creating this new society.

For a decade and a half after the ending of the War virtually all Christian denominations enjoyed a remarkable period of growth throughout North America. As the Canadian church historian, John Grant Webster, has observed, "Men and women who had shown no more than a perfunctory interest in the church before going off to war demonstrated on their return an enthusiasm that confounded all prognosticators."[1] Every aspect of church life—membership, lay activity, vocations for the ministry, financial givings, erecting buildings, reading religious literature—showed an extraordinary increase. The massive wave of immigration that poured into Canada in this period, much of it destined for southern Ontario, fuelled this phenomenon.

What accounted for such an incredible growth in church membership? Grant argues that,

> In retrospect it seems obvious that the sobering experiences of the depression and war had raised questions for which many Canadians

> would ultimately seek answers from the churches. Although wartime discussions of theology had little immediate effect on church attendance, their ultimate effect was to persuade many uncommitted people that Christianity deserved to be taken seriously.[2]

Similarly, educational leaders were challenged by the demands of this changing Canadian society. At the end of the War they inherited a dilapidated physical structure that had not been improved since the early 1930s. The low birthrate of the Depression and War years had militated against the need for more buildings. Because many teachers and administrators had served in the armed services or war industries, boards had been forced to recruit many poorly trained people. And, by the end of the War, many educators and politicians were criticizing the curriculum. Was it adequate to prepare children for post-war society? Were children being equipped to fill the employment opportunities that were emerging in industrial Canada? Much of this criticism was directed against the secondary-school programme, which critics said placed too much emphasis on the traditional subjects.

Aware of these criticisms and of his earlier promise to conduct a sweeping review of the province's public educational system, Premier Drew announced the appointment of a Royal Commission in March, 1945 under the chairmanship of Mr. Justice John Hope. Townshend, along with 20 other individuals—both professional educators and lay people—were appointed to this group. As one commentator noted, this varied composition "meant twenty-one opinions on every subject. And since they represented different geographic areas and different schools of thought, the amazing thing is not that they took so long to arrive at their conclusions, but that they were able to arrive at any generally accepted conclusions at all."[3]

Why was Townshend selected to serve on this commission? Two reasons can be offered. First, he had already acquired a considerable reputation as a trustee with advanced views on the nature of education and the role of the public school system, of which, as has been pointed out, he was a stout and outspoken champion. Secondly, there was his intimate connection with the Conservative Party and, in this sense, it was basically a matter of party patronage.[4]

At the outset of their labours this diverse group displayed a large degree of unanimity. Certainly their terms of reference gave them ample scope. They were authorized to investigate every facet of the public system from kindergarten to the end of secondary education, including textbooks, curriculum, examinations, financing and the administrative structure.[5] The commission eagerly got down to business, anticipating that it would probably submit its report within a year or so. If reforms were needed, the government wanted to undertake them as quickly as possible. The commission immediately set a rapid and demanding pace for its members. Within a year it had held approximately 150 public hearings, mostly in Toronto, although it also sat in other centres and read 258 briefs submitted by various organizations and individuals. Obviously there was intense interest in the commission's work and, in light of many of the submissions, a desire to introduce real changes in the public educational system. The omens were bright for a new start to public education, and there was high anticipation that the commission would respond to this challenge. But that, as it turned out, was not to be the case!

Townshend, in typical fashion, threw himself into the commission's work, for here was a splendid opportunity to publicize and push his views on education. It really was the chance of a lifetime. The commission established a number of sub-committees to investigate various issues. Not unnaturally he was chosen to be chairman of the committee whose task was to review the financial structure of the school system and to try to design a new method of financing public education so that it might be less burdensome for property holders. After all, Premier Drew had promised that the province would ultimately shoulder 60 per cent of the total cost of education. That certainly was a spur to Townshend's group to devise something new!

Since the commission met so often in Toronto, Townshend was able to sandwich these meetings in between those of many General Synod boards and committees. Often he stayed overnight but usually he tried to make that last train to London.

While the commission was carrying out its work, Townshend, of course, was still immersed in the details of local education in London. Obtaining teachers and building new facilities were immediate pressing concerns in the post-war era, as the vanguard of what became known as the "baby boom" began entering Grade 1. Related to these problems was the ever thorny issue of finances. Even though the government had revised the grant system in 1945, trustees were still scrambling to find sources of revenue to cover their increasing expenses.[6]

Townshend canvassed all of these problems in his inaugural address when he assumed the chairmanship of the London Board in January, 1946.[7] His most immediate concern was trying to attract the best-qualified teachers for the city's schools. London, he warned, needed to move quickly as other boards were offering financial inducements to prospective teachers. Then he described the other salient issues facing the board. The city's rapidly expanding population necessitated building more schools over the next few years. Even though construction materials were still scarce, the board, he reported, had already advocated securing more property before land prices rose. Here was the kernel of his scheme to stockpile land for future development. He predicted that London's school enrollment would experience continuous growth for the next five years. The prophecy was wildly off the mark! But he was not alone in mistaking the remarkable demographic surge about to hit Canadian society.

Of the other issues he touched upon, it was his reference to the Royal Commission that was most significant. He informed his colleagues that a brief was being composed for submission but, since the commission would probably not be reporting for some time (here his prognostication was deadly accurate), he suggested the board seek the Department's permission to implement some of the reforms of the secondary-school programme that had been mooted in London during the past few years. London, he hoped, might become a laboratory for working out his own ideas. Of course, as we know, Townshend had a vested interest in these proposals. Not only had he been advocating them for a decade, but he had, in the previous year, been chairman of the curriculum committee which had composed the board's brief for the commission.

For the rest of 1946, and for many years to come, the problems he described in this address became the staple of board deliberations. Galvanized by Townshend, the trustees set to work. The salary schedule was revised, raising the minimum and maximum levels, although a differential still existed between male and female teachers. Plans for new schools were drawn up, especially for one along the city's eastern border where much of the increase in population was taking place. A start was made on creating materials for the new high-school courses. Within a year, however, the Department imposed a moratorium on further curriculum development, asking the boards to wait until the commission had reported.

Even with the increasing enrollment, Townshend tried to persuade the board to reduce the size of classes in the interests of both better working conditions and improved learning environments for the children. But the rush of pupils into the schools soon prevented this move.[8] However, the board did make a start on establishing a pension plan for the non-teaching staff—another of Townshend's pet projects. By the end of his chairmanship a fund of 15,000 dollars had been set aside for this purpose.[9]

LONDON'S TRUSTEES, AS indicated, were as interested in the potential of the Hope Commission as any group in the province. Here was a major public forum where they could advertise the interesting ideas and innovations they had been experimenting with for the past few years. So the group was ready to present its views when Justice Hope gavelled the meeting to order on the morning of February 19, 1946. The vice-chairman of the board, Miss Evelyn Harrison, briefly introduced the board's document, emphasizing that it had been composed by both trustees and teachers. It was left to Dr. G.A. Wheable, superintendent of schools, to present and defend it. The brief covered a number of topics, but its central core focussed on needed revisions to the secondary-school programme. Drawing on London's experience with its own innovative approach, Wheable outlined several changes which the board contended would improve the educational development of adolescents and enhance their employment opportunities. Specifically, the brief called for a reduction in the number of required courses in Grade 9, thereby allowing "more time for student work and independent thinking."[10] Since many students did not have adequate study facilities at home, the document suggested lengthening the school day by an hour or an hour-and-a-half so that pupils could complete their assignments before leaving for the day.

However, it was a wholesale revision of the collegiate curriculum that was the most startling part of this brief. To accommodate the needs of the very large number of adolescents who had no desire to attend university, the London group recommended opening a third type of secondary school. Called the Modern School, it would stand alongside the collegiate institute and the vocational school.[11] Preparation for practical living was to be its aim; inculcating skills for everyday living lay at the heart of its programme. Eleven subjects were listed as constituting this new curriculum. Civics, for example, would stress the duties of a citizen and the responsibility to vote, and would offer an explanation of current events. Science would concentrate on teaching students to become familiar with the problems of heating, lighting and ventilation in homes. Instruction in cooking, child care, making a budget, choosing insurance plans, negotiating mortgages, and other facets of modern living would be taught to both sexes in a new Housekeeping course.

This set of recommendations was certainly a refreshing breath of air in Ontario secondary education. Whatever may be said about the origins of the London group's brief, it was novel. What this board was really calling for was secondary education for all adolescents in a day when most teenagers left high school to seek employment as soon as they could. A high-school education was not regarded by the majority of society as a necessity. But here was a group advocating a veritable revolution in the public's attitude. As it turned out, many years passed before the Ontario government advocated this idea, but the seeds for it were planted in 1946, and no one was more responsible than Townshend.

Dr. Wheable defended the brief and handled many queries and criticisms from the commissioners, many of whom displayed an intense interest in this scheme. Only once did Townshend himself intervene, and that was to focus more attention on the Modern School. He keenly wanted his fellow commissioners to understand the need for the Modern School, and he earnestly hoped the commission would include it in their final recommendations.[12]

The London brief was not the only one with which Townshend was associated. The Anglican Provincial Synod also submitted one, for which he acted as a consultant.[13] As might be expected, the role of religious education in the public school system was the principal concern of this brief. The bishops cautioned the government to remain vigilant in fending off attempts to reduce or remove religious instruction. After all, as the brief correctly noted, Christian denominations had played a significant role in the formation of the province's public school system, and it would be a denial of the past if this subject were withdrawn.

At the very end of their submission the Synod called for a revision of the high-school curriculum, suggesting that students not going on to university be allowed to take "a larger number of elective courses."[14] These ecclesiastics, however, did not feel competent to specify any particular subjects. Undoubtedly, the recommendation for electives was inserted at Townshend's behest. It had all the earmarks of his handiwork. Moreover, he was determined that the commission would hear this idea from as many sources as he could muster.

In September, the commission spent several days traversing northern Ontario, hearing testimony on the particular educational problems of this area. By going there, the commission hoped to offset the north's feeling that this region was generally neglected by Toronto. Certainly it proved to be an eye-opening experience for Townshend. In Timmins the local inspector, a Mr. Brown, delivered a devastating critique of the deplorable conditions of many of the area's schools. Townshend, who had visited one of them, publicly supported Brown's comments. "Mr. Brown is correct in his estimate of the situation," the Timmins *Daily Press* reported Townshend as saying. "Conditions where I visited were terrible. I could put my hand through the holes in the wall."[15] In all, the commissioners spent just over a week in the north, but at no other place did they find a similar situation.

Townshend's involvement with education in 1946 reached a climax in November. The board had set aside the first week of this month to enlighten the public about what was being done in their schools. "Education for the Atomic Age" was the theme chosen for the week. A number of activities were planned to try to heighten the public's perception of the need for a more diversified education. One of Townshend's main contributions to this effort was a speech he made over radio CFPL on the evening of November 7. Taking as his topic the need for schools to teach international brotherhood in this age of atomic peril, he warned his hearers that the methods and curriculum of the little red schoolhouse were no longer sufficient. An education that trained youth to be self-sufficient and that placed God at the centre of human activities was urgently required. Such an approach, he admonished, needed

> ...leaders in education with courage to act beyond the pulse of public opinion. It needs officials who recognize youth in training and potential man in action. It needs teachers who understand that a subject and a textbook are merely means to an end. Christian principles are stronger than personal desires. It needs a public consciousness that youth lives in a world of its own but a world where adult approval and assistance are as welcome as love and affection.[16]

This address was not only a cry for a revised curriculum but a plea for the public to regard education as an essential ingredient in the creation of a society that would be free from the perils of the nuclear age.

EXPANSION AND ITS attendant problems were also on the Church's agenda that year. And, since he was still the Diocesan Commissioner, Townshend was deeply immersed in them. Aside from the Diocesan Forward Campaign, which has been described, two other major issues confronted him. One was the National Church's financial drive and the other was the need to erect more churches to accommodate the burgeoning population. General Synod's campaign, the Anglican Advance Appeal (A.A.A.), set a target of four million dollars. Of this sum, the Diocese of Huron was asked to raise 497,000 dollars. Townshend was drafted to serve on the national committee, which meant he had to attend more meetings in Toronto and, hence, was away even more from his family. Occasionally, he had to travel to other cities across the country as the group often met in other localities. Consequently, he was not deeply involved in the local effort, although he helped to organize deanery committees and assisted some congregations in training canvassers.

Within a year the Archbishop joyfully announced that the diocese had oversubscribed its target.[17] Three years had been allotted to complete the effort. Seager advised the committee to collect these pledges as quickly as possible while the laity's enthusiasm was still high. Consequently, follow-up committees were appointed and, along with his myriad responsibilities, Townshend was placed in charge of this effort in two deaneries located in the northern and western sections of the diocese. Huron benefited greatly from the national campaign as well, because each diocese was guaranteed to receive part of the total sum raised within its boundaries. Huron's share, together with the money raised in its own Forward Campaign, certainly gave it a reasonably solid financial base from which to launch its post-war programmes.

Church extension was the other major issue with which Townshend had to deal that year. Actually, discussions concerning the erecting of more churches had begun during the War. A Church Extension Committee, with Principal O'Neil of Huron College as its convenor and with Townshend as a member, had been appointed in 1943. This group, in turn, had set up extension committees in each deanery to survey their local needs, but very little had been achieved before the end of the War. In fact, many members of the executive committee were reluctant to spend money at this time, and Townshend often faced bitter opposition to his plans to purchase property in sparsely populated areas which he forecast would be settled after the War. These conflicts gave rise to one episode which over time was virtually transformed into a legend. The Gartshore estate on the city's southern edge came on the market, and Townshend, sensing a good deal, wanted the committee to buy a part of it. The members summarily rejected his pleas. Feeling very strongly that this was a good site for a future church building, he made a down payment with his own funds. When the United Church showed an interest in the land, Townshend warned the executive group that if they didn't secure it immediately, he would relinquish his claim, "and I shall leave here [the committee meeting] a happy man because I stand to make a great deal of money."[18] The committee got the message, and swiftly released the necessary funds. In later years, St. Andrew's Memorial Church was built on this spot.

While the really concerted drive for church extension took place during the episcopate of George Luxton (who was elected bishop in 1948 and will be treated later), certainly a beginning was made in 1946. London's committee, chaired by Canon A.A. Trumper, wrote a report for the archbishop which recommended purchasing sites close to where new schools were planned. This group had relied upon Townshend for such information. The committee's report sounded a note that was echoed countless times in the next few years:

> Our visitation impressed us with the unparalleled development taking place within this City and on its borders, and we affirm our belief that it all presented the greatest challenge that has been presented to the Church in London in this generation. May we have grace to rise to the occasion, and by Divine guidance avoid the mistakes of the past.[19]

What this committee discovered in London, others found in many other parts of the diocese.

These manifold activities placed a heavy strain on the diocese's leadership. The principal administrators were growing old and, perhaps, were not mentally prepared to handle the challenges facing them. Both Archbishop Seager and Archdeacon Doherty, the secretary-treasurer, were in their 70s, had health problems, and were becoming weary of their daily tasks. When Doherty finally retired in 1947, Townshend was chosen to take his place.[20] He was the obvious choice, and Doherty himself was anxious that Townshend be his successor. Townshend slipped easily into his new position. His duties were considerably different from being Diocesan Commissioner. Now he was in total control of the finances, since he was responsible for drafting the annual budget, setting the parochial apportionment figures, and handling the diocese's investments. No longer was he expected to travel around the diocese settling disputes. Yet he still attended deanery meetings to explain the Church's financial needs. Together with his work on the Royal Commission, it meant he was still absent from home much of the time, leaving Kathleen to look after the domestic scene.

In every year that Townshend served as secretary-treasurer, the budget target figure was over-subscribed. Each year until he left this office in 1955, he reported to Synod that the diocese had exceeded the required amount by anywhere from 104 to 108 per cent. Many clergy and laity, however, felt that he was too heavy-handed in his methods of raising money and that this endeavour was over-shadowing the Church's spiritual efforts. No doubt at times he did appear to be driven by a fierce need to accumulate money, and it seemed as if this was the major thrust of his ministry. But, in fairness to him, it must be recalled that he had been given the task of bringing order to the diocese's finances. Both the Depression and the War had forced the Church, like other institutions, to scrape and scrimp in order to provide even the most basic services. Furthermore, as noted, the post-war era was a very prosperous one, and Townshend felt that the Church must capitalize on this situation. Money was needed for the increasing burden of church extension and other new activities the diocese was contemplating. Without adequate funding, the programmes could not be mounted.

IN SEPTEMBER, 1948, OLD Archbishop Seager died. Immediately, a special session of Synod was convened to elect a successor. There were two obvious candidates, Townshend and Dean George Luxton. Luxton had entered the diocese in 1944 and had quickly become a favourite with many local laymen. Yet, as the "local boy" who had done so much for the diocese, Townshend might have been regarded as the favourite choice. However, he placed second to Luxton in the ensuing election, and thus missed becoming the father-in-God to his old diocese.[21] Naturally, he was disappointed. Part of the reason for Luxton's success was the support he received from some prominent laymen who actively canvassed on his behalf. Perhaps Townshend's importuning for money had turned some of the electors against him.

Swallowing his disappointment, Townshend immediately pledged his support to the new diocesan bishop. In retrospect, this was an ironic act. Very soon Luxton and Townshend found it difficult to work together. Partly this is explained as a clash of two strong personalities; but they also had genuine differences of opinion about various aspects of church policy, especially church extension. Luxton was a builder; he was avid to erect new churches in every conceivable area of southwest Ontario. Townshend, on the other hand, while he recognized the growing need for more buildings, adopted a more cautious approach. "George Luxton would build a church on every corner of the diocese if he could," Townshend once commented.[22]

Other issues needed attention at the moment, and none was more pressing than securing a new building for Huron College. The old one had outlived its usefulness. Property had been purchased on Western Road opposite the university, and College Council was anxious to erect a building there. Selling the old site became a thorny proposition for Townshend. The council, hoping to raise funds quickly, was quite willing to dispose of it at a low price. Townshend was astounded. Claiming that he could obtain twice the amount the council had set, he persuaded the board to leave the sale totally in his hands. Quickly he secured a much higher price but in a very unusual manner. An enterprising young man came forward with a scheme to build apartments on the land, but frankly indicated that he lacked sufficient funds for a large down-payment. Townshend intuitively felt that this man was a good risk, and so approached the board with this offer. The council, reluctantly bowing to Townshend's persuasion, accepted the proposal. After changing the board's mind, he then helped the purchaser to secure a loan from a financial institution to cover the down-payment and construction costs. Within two years the apartments had been erected, and had earned enough money for the man to discharge the entire mortgage. In some measure this episode dispels the notion that in making real-estate deals Townshend was motivated solely by the opportunity to make a profit. His faith in this man's integrity and ability were amply repaid.[23]

Although Townshend was involved in the campaign to raise funds for the new building, the leadership of the drive was largely in the hands of others. The details of this effort have been recounted elsewhere and need not be repeated here.[24]

Another aspect of the college's life in these years that drew Townshend's interest was the appointment of a new principal. In 1952, O'Neil resigned to assume the position of field secretary for the British and Foreign Bible Society. One of the leading candidates for the office was the Rev. W. Coleman, a professor at Bishop's University, Lennoxville, Quebec. Coleman was a very able man, but somewhere Townshend had been told that Coleman had acquired high-church tendencies. This would not do at Huron College. Townshend, anxious to preserve the evangelical purity of his *alma mater*, boldly asked the candidate's father about his son's theological stance. Having been assured that his information was incorrect, Townshend became a major supporter of Coleman, who became the successful candidate.[25]

While he was caught up in these activities, Townshend's family was growing, entering the professions, marrying, and having children. The registers of the Church of the Redeemer record these marriages and the baptisms of the grandchildren. As he was still absent from home a great deal of the time, it was becoming more difficult than ever to be involved with his expanding family.

Although he had not been a parish priest for many years, people still sought his assistance for a variety of things. Townshend, as many clergy reported, was an extremely approachable person, and his correspondence records many appeals for help, especially by applicants seeking teaching positions. Usually he advised these people to send their applications to administrators whose names he supplied. Occasionally, he cheerfully wrote a letter of reference for someone he knew. Perhaps the most poignant requests he received in these years were those from people attempting to secure parole from prison sentences. One young lad who had been a choir boy at the Church of the Redeemer (and then later at the cathedral) sought Townshend's help. Unfortunately, the boy had broken a previous parole. Townshend warned him that this action could earn him an extended sentence, and advised him to settle down and lead a more responsible life. However, this advice was rejected and the lad was sentenced to another jail term. Townshend, saddened by this outcome, told the prison chaplain, "I had hopes of his some day becoming a good man. I feel that it is in him to become such, but he seems determined to go the wrong way."[26] There were other episodes of a similar nature. Townshend's faith in people and his incurable optimism constantly drove him to try to help them even though the results were often disappointing.

On the other hand, there were occasions when his efforts paid off. In one year he achieved three notable successes for teachers, students, and other employees of the Board of Education. After many years of ignoring his pleas for a pension scheme for caretakers, the London board adopted one in 1947. Also adopted was a system of sabbatical leaves for teachers, a cause which he had long advocated.[27] Finally, he was also successful in persuading the board to hire an itinerant teacher to help children afflicted with cerebral palsy.

Equally important for education in London was the continuous growth of London's population. The southern extremity of the city was rapidly being settled, and consequently new school buildings were desperately needed. By 1949 a new school, named Princess Elizabeth, had been erected for this area. At the same time another new one, Knollwood Park, was being built in the eastern region. The board decided to hold the opening ceremonies for both schools on the same day, taking advantage of the occasion to make it a major public relations event. The Lieutenant-Governor of Ontario, the Hon. Ray Lawson, a native of London, was invited to conduct ceremonies at both openings. Townshend, who was in charge of the one at Princess Elizabeth School, seized the opportunity not only to impress upon the audience the need for these new buildings but also to emphasize how these buildings incorporated the most recent advances in school construction.

FOR MANY YEARS Townshend had been very active in provincial trustee organizations. In 1949 he was elected president of the Public School Trustees Association of Ontario. This group had been organized in 1939 at the behest of the Toronto board to protect the public system "against new and renewed demands to undermine and weaken the great common school system of Ontario."[28] Coming shortly after the Liberal government's attempts to increase funding for Roman Catholic Separate Schools, it was not difficult to fathom who the enemy was! This campaign, of course, was one dear to Townshend's heart, and he eagerly lent his support.

In his presidential address he paid tribute to the necessity of a public system and warned that "there are forces about that would destroy this Great Public School System."[29] No doubt this oblique remark was directed at Rome. However, he concentrated his remarks on three major themes. He began by iterating his old argument that the essential purpose of education was to prepare youth for abundant living. He bluntly dismissed the notion that schools existed to train students for employment. "An education system that fits people only for jobs is failing in its purposes," was his retort to such a limited vision.[30]

What did he mean by "abundant living"? In trying to define this phrase he linked it to the characteristics of the new age he saw emerging. Life had become more complex than in the past. A new style of education, he claimed, was necessary to help adolescents prepare for such a world. What were the hallmarks of this new approach? The individual child must now receive more attention; emphasizing course content had to be relegated to second place. Flowing from this premise Townshend called for a de-emphasis on marks. "I visualize schools where the measure of a student is not the marks he makes on an examination but the progress he makes in self-development; where the incentive to study is not the possibility of failure in a subject, but the happiness found in doing that which springs from the source of interest and providing a sense of achievement."[31] Only a curriculum that "challenged his [the pupil's] potential and that fitted him for constructive self-expression in the community" could achieve this result.[32]

Introducing such a programme was a challenge for both teachers and trustees. Here was his second theme. Teachers in this era had to develop a wider vision of their profession. The emotional and spiritual needs of their students must receive equal attention with the intellectual side. In a word, "they will need to know how to use a subject, text or otherwise, for the interpretation of life and for the building of character; they must realize that book knowledge and accepted methodology are not enough."[33]

Equally trustees must accept a new role. Their task was to instruct the public about the requirements of modern education. Ideally, board members should become the leaders of educational progress in their areas. Townshend felt it was imperative for trustees to be constantly in touch with parents, preparing them for the benefits that were about to flow from new ideas and programmes.

It was a very wide-ranging speech, in which he reiterated and fleshed out many of the proposals he had been advocating for years. Much of the address was couched in highly idealistic terms, but he made no apology for this:

> Ideals are important in days of cold realism, and in holding up an ideal (especially one that is quite within our reach) I am attempting to lift our eyes from the multitudinous details of our duties in order that progress may be speeded up and ultimate achievement of abundant living for our boys and girls brought nearer. Let us, therefore, as trustees, officials, teachers and parents, strive to do a full part in developing in our boys and girls an enriched personality for service.[34]

Ironically, this speech provoked a spirited attack on Townshend's integrity by one of his fellow commissioners. Mr. Henry St. Jacques of Ottawa claimed that Townshend had divulged many of the proposals that the commission was considering. Stung by this attack, Townshend lashed back at St. Jacques. "No commissioner has more jealously guarded the secrets of the commission than I have," he angrily retorted. Why, he hadn't even told Kathleen what the commission was contemplating. "I am grieved that a fellow commissioner has accorded such treatment to a fellow member for either [sic] by word or deed have I betrayed a confidence of the commission."[35] Certainly it was a nasty exchange and drew a cloud over the commission's work.

This was one of the last public episodes for the Hope Commission. It was now time to write the report. Again, it was anticipated that this would be a relatively short task, after which the government could begin to implement the recommendations. However, as noted, this was not to be. (Four years were to pass before the commission finally submitted its report.) Immediately the 21 individuals with their diverse opinions and beliefs began to squabble and bicker among themselves, making it difficult to reach a consensus. Several times the government announced that the final product was forthcoming, only to be disappointed once more. The press was constantly haranguing the commission to publish. Time was passing, and as the enrollment problem began to burgeon, it was becoming more and more difficult for the government and the boards to remain excited about what those commissioners might recommend. In spite of the severe criticism from so many sources, the commissioners continued in their leisurely fashion. One of the tragic mistakes of this commission, for which they were severely criticized at the time, was not issuing one or more interim reports. At the very least such previews would have kept the public and educators informed of the kind of thinking and the proposals the commission was discussing.

Finally the report was finished! After five years of hearing briefs, travelling around the country (for some of the commissioners this meant trips outside of Canada to view foreign systems), attending sub-committee meetings, and enduring interminable wrangling among the commissioners—and there had been much of that—the commission submitted its recommendations in a huge tome of 930 pages. Nor was it written in the most inspiring prose. In a public setting, Justice Hope presented the report to Premier Frost on December 22, 1950—an incredibly inauspicious time of the year! The government was aghast at what it read. The report was a political time bomb. Frost, who had never approved of the commission, arguing that its terms of reference were too broad, quickly moved to shelve it. As he told one of his old friends in Orillia, "The great difficulty with this Report is that in many respects it lacks any real relationship to reality."[36]

Here was another kind of criticism levelled at the report: it was politically naive. Two or three of its principal recommendations (and it made over 300) were dynamite, especially its call for a reorganization of the school system by reducing the primary level from eight years to six. To Roman Catholic leaders this was simply a blatant attempt to undermine the Separate Schools. Hope's group did not seem to understand the importance of the constitutional safeguards granted to the Roman Catholic School system at the time of Confederation. Both the reorganization scheme and the apparent attack on the Separate Schools frightened the government, and it quickly backed away from the report. In an editorial the *Globe and Mail* labelled the report a "Tragedy of Errors". On the one day that the government allotted for discussion of the report in the legislature, it was treated as a laughing matter.[37] The report was born dead!

Townshend was dismayed at the government's reaction. Here, he argued, was an opportunity to introduce many needed changes into the province's education system at a critical moment. In what seemed to him a hasty move, the Premier threw away a promising opportunity simply because one or two minority groups disliked a few of the report's suggestions.

One commentator has suggested that although the report was "barren on the surface, the Hope Commission has given life to many later developments in the province's educational system."[38] Indeed, most of the issues considered by this commission surfaced again in the 1960s. In many ways, it set the agenda for educational debate for the next 15 to 20 years. One unhappy result was to dissuade future Ontario governments from using the royal commission technique as a means of reforming its schools. When most other provinces appointed commissions to review their school structures in the 1960s, Ontario's Department of Education resorted to appointing small committees, usually composed of professional educators only, to investigate and make recommendations on single issues rather than more sweeping ones. Even the highly touted Hall-Dennis Committee, whose work will be noted later, originally had restricted terms of reference. The failure of the Hope Commission cast a pall on educational innovation in Ontario for a decade.

WHAT WAS THERE in the report that reflected Townshend's thoughts on education? Many years later he told a correspondent, "My educational philosophy has not changed since the Report was submitted. I think that philosophy is well outlined in chapter 2 of the Report."[39] This chapter set forth the commission's aims and objectives for the system. They were a mixture of traditional and progressive attitudes and, not unnaturally for the time, contained numerous references to the place of Christianity in Ontario's society. Echoing many of the ideas Townshend had uttered for years, the commissioners argued that the school's most important function was to impart a sense of honesty and Christian love in young people. Character development and instilling the "cardinal virtues" were the central purposes of public education. Yet, the current curriculum was too narrow to achieve the manifold aims which the commission had espoused. Schools for the modern world needed to be learner experiences not simply book learning, and they must attempt to educate the whole child. None of this was new. It had become the common place language of educators all over the continent during the previous five or six decades. But it was certainly novel, if not startling, to read it in a royal commission report.

How were these aims to be achieved? The commission's prescription was to carry out "a somewhat radical revision of our present system of education."[40] While the commissioners may have thought that their suggestions were radical for Ontario, many other areas of North America had introduced similar ones years ago. Basically, the commission wanted to revise the number of years allotted to each section of the school system. In their design the primary level would cover the first six years, and secondary school would be reduced to four years by eliminating Grade 13. Beyond this level, a system of junior colleges would be established to prepare students either for university entrance or employment. The commission attempted to justify this scheme by basing it on the findings of developmental psychology.

While the government shied away from this proposal, Townshend strongly endorsed it. "I was vitally interested in the reorganization of our whole system, and I still feel we were on the right track in our recommendations," he later told a correspondent.[41] Certainly the suggested programme was very different from the fare currently offered by the collegiates.[42] While a core of subjects would still remain at the heart of the secondary-school curriculum, the commission recommended that many new courses, such as home economics, shop work, cadet training, and others, be offered. These subjects had never been regarded as part of a necessary education in Ontario. Obviously, the commission wanted to broaden the high school's offerings and make it more relevant for an expanded student body. To this end, the commission recommended the introduction of a limited credit system in the final two years of high school. The intent was to permit students to take courses which interested them and perhaps would entice them to stay longer.

All of these proposed changes were expensive. The financing of education was, of course, one of Townshend's major interests. He had spent years wrestling with this issue in London, and had tried to encourage trustees to use their resources in a responsible and efficient manner. As chairman of the commission's sub-committee on finances, he had an opportunity to spread his message around the province and, at the same time, to seek new methods of securing funds for education.

Two chapters of the report dealt with this matter. After reviewing the historical development of funding for public education, the commission set forth its proposals for a new and different approach. The property tax would remain as the principal source of revenue on the local level, but a novel twist was introduced by suggesting that for public and separate elementary schools only property owned by individuals should be taxed. Taxes collected from property belonging to corporations and public utilities would be used to support high schools. The objective behind this approach was to avoid the contentious argument about Separate Schools sharing in this source. Needless to say, this suggestion became a part of the larger argument about Separate Schools. The commission also called for a province-wide system of property assessment to make the financing of schools more equitable across the province. But the government's refusal to accept the commission's report scuppered all of these proposals, although many of them surfaced in the next decade and were implemented.

Were all of the commission's recommendations summarily rejected? One study, written six years after the report's submission, claimed that 100 of its more than 300 proposals were implemented either wholly or in part.[43] Townshend felt that even more than this number had been adopted. He told one individual who inquired about this matter that he and Dr. J.G. Althouse, the former Director of Education for Ontario, had spent four hours one day pouring over the report attempting to discern the final outcome of its suggestions. "We were most agreeably surprised to learn that more than two hundred of the three hundred or so recommendations had been implemented, in full or in part. I feel that is a very good batting average for any Royal Commission."[44]

And indeed it was! But still, as with so many royal commissions, its participants were unhappy with the final outcome. Townshend, who ever after regarded his work on the commission as one of the highlights of his educational activities, was particularly disappointed that the government, and a Conservative one at that, had not endorsed it. He saw incredible benefits both for the children and the province in the multitude of recommendations. Ironically, when many of them were implemented during the following decade, the report and its authors received very little credit for their work.

IN THE MIDST OF THIS controversy over the Hope Commission, Townshend continued to wrestle with the problems facing the local board. In 1951 he was again elected chairman and, as was the custom, he delivered an inaugural speech. Much of the early part of it was a recapitulation of his address to the trustee's association in the previous year. Then he got down to the pressing issues facing the London board. Salary negotiations with both the teaching and non-teaching staff, recruiting more teachers, finding more classrooms, and the impact of the city's growing population, coupled with the possibility that the city might annex sections of the county—all were placed on the board's agenda.

London, like so many urban centres in Ontario, was facing educational challenges that were approaching crisis proportion. One of these was teachers' demands for increased salaries. Townshend wanted this matter settled quickly.[45] Early in January the board offered a series of raises to all groups but, as usual, many months passed before an agreement was reached, only to have the process begin again.

In fact, negotiations about teachers' salaries, benefits and working conditions were becoming more demanding, and none more so than those involving the Ontario Secondary School Teachers' Federation (O.S.S.T.F.). This was the year in which the O.S.S.T.F. leadership led a strike against the Kirkland Lake board and invoked a newly devised technique called the pink list. This device prevented teachers from applying for any position with a board that was so listed. Trustees across the province, alarmed at this development, began to discuss the possibility of banding together to provide a counterweight to the growing power of the federations. Townshend, while sympathizing with the teachers' desires to improve their material lot, regarded this growing militancy with a degree of uneasiness. Confrontation was not his style.

However, the issue was resolved for the moment, and London, as always, reached an amicable settlement with its staff.

Securing sufficient classroom space became another major headache for London's trustees that year, as it would be for the next two decades. Townshend warned the board that the current enrollment in kindergarten exceeded that of Grade 8 by 400. Not only would this require hiring more teachers for the fall term, but the burgeoning enrollment required more space immediately. And, furthermore, the city's scheme to annex land along its eastern border, if successful, would only exacerbate this problem. Many of the small boards in the area faced a similar enrollment challenge. London had worked out a sharing arrangement with some of them, permitting their students to attend city schools. Others had begun to erect new buildings. Townshend feared that the city might become responsible for these small schools if annexation were accomplished. He asked his fellow trustees to try to persuade their township counterparts to delay any new construction for at least a year until the annexation issue had been settled.[46] As it turned out, the process of securing more land dragged on for virtually a decade, with London acquiring small parcels in the area until it made its final addition in the early 1960s. However, this slow acquisition policy left the small boards of the region free to build schools, and their existence became a major problem when full annexation did occur in 1961.

In the meantime, the London board resorted to a number of expedients which became common practice over the years. A few rooms were reopened in a recently closed school, while others in a new building that was still under construction were hastily fitted out. Classrooms were added to four existing schools. Two of these, Knollwood Park and Princess Elizabeth, had been opened only two years earlier—a clear demonstration of the extent of the enrollment problem.[47] Even these efforts were not sufficient; space had to be rented in church halls and other institutions in a mad race to keep pace with the city's growth.

In the midst of these pressing demands, which must have made the trustees feel that they were simply scrambling to survive, Townshend was pleased to inform the board of a major development. This was the opening in London of the Educational Clinic under the direction of the assistant superintendent of schools. Its function was to assist children and adolescents whose emotional or psychological problems prevented them from making satisfactory progress in school. Townshend, who had always been keenly interested in such children, had long advocated some form of special education for them. In its first year, the clinic served a large number of children, offering them a variety of remedies, including special remedial classes opened at St. George's school. Townshend, proud of this achievement, boasted to the board at the end of the year that, "In the time in which it has been operating, this clinic has achieved very worthwhile results."[48]

AS WE KNOW, TOWNSHEND had for many years been deeply involved with the work of the National Church. One of the highlights of church involvement for many Anglican clergy and laity is participating in sessions of the General Synod, the Church's highest legislative body. Meeting in different centres across the country, it gave delegates a broader perspective on many aspects of the Church's activities. Huron had hosted these sessions twice before, in 1911 and 1924, and was chosen again for the 1952 conference. Months of work went into preparing for the event. Billets for those attending were secured at Huron College and in private homes around the city; rooms for meetings were obtained from the university; laity and local clergy were recruited for innumerable tasks. All was in readiness when the more than 300 delegates began to arrive on September, 1952 for ten days of discussions.

The colourful opening service was conducted at the cathedral on the evening of September 4th with the Very Rev. W.R. Matthews, Dean of St. Paul's Cathedral, London, England, as the guest preacher. The Dean brought with him a gift from his cathedral—a piece of marble from the high altar which had been destroyed in a bombing raid during the War. It was set in a prominent place in the Huron cathedral.

The next morning the Primate, Archbishop Barfoot of Edmonton, delivered his charge to the assembled delegates, after which the major departments and committees began to submit their reports for scrutiny. Townshend was principally concerned with the work of two groups—the Budget and the Primatial See Committees. The former was still trying to devise an equitable apportionment scheme, and noted that a sub-committee, headed by Townshend, had spent four years grappling with this issue. Townshend's group had submitted a table of figures to serve as guidelines for negotiating with the dioceses about the amounts each one felt it could contribute towards the General Synod's work. The committee clearly realized that among the several factors which affected a diocese's ability to pay, none was more significant than the individual parishioner's willingness to contribute. In a blunt statement the report argued that, "When we bring the willingness-to-pay [sic] of our people up to their ability to pay, we shall have solved the financial problems of the church."[49] Here was the heart of the matter. Anglicans, as a recent study had shown, were not good givers, and needed to be persuaded to donate more money for the Church's increasing responsibilities.

For 20 years, General Synod had been seeking a solution to the question of where to locate a primate after he had been elected. Since only archbishops and diocesan bishops were eligible for this office, the successful candidate brought with him diocesan (and often metropolitan) responsibilities. It was strongly felt that the primate should retain some connection with a diocese. This was a heavy burden, further increased by the need to spend time at the Church's national headquarters located in Toronto. For Archbishop Barfoot, who was also head of the Edmonton diocese, the situation was almost intolerable. Various solutions had been proposed during the previous two decades, the most popular being the creation of a small primatial see in downtown Toronto with St. Paul's Church, Bloor Street, as the cathedral.

Townshend had been made a member of this committee at the Synod of 1949. During the interval it had met several times, trying to seek a satisfactory resolution. In its submission the committee stated that the establishment of a fixed see "at the present time is inopportune."[50] Since the current arrangement placed such a severe strain on Barfoot, the group recommended that he limit his visits to other dioceses to a few per year and that Edmonton be asked to grant him an episcopal assistant. During the ensuing debate on the floor of Synod, Townshend pleaded with members to decide the issue one way or the other, but his efforts were fruitless.[51] This question was not resolved for many years, when it was finally decided to place the primate in Toronto, shorn of any diocesan duties.

The delegates were not kept "locked up" in sessions all the time. Several social events were held, and the diocese sponsored an elaborate pageant, entitled "Even Our Faith", to commemorate the 50th anniversary of the M.S.C.C. Involving dozens of local people, it was a clever depiction of the history of the Church of England in Canada. On Sunday morning, the bishops, clergy, and many laymen fanned out to parishes around the diocese as special preachers, telling the faithful of Huron about the work of the Church in their areas, including, in some cases, overseas regions. In the afternoon Bishop Luxton spoke about the work of General Synod on the C.B.C. program, "Church of the Air", which was broadcast from the Church of St. John the Evangelist in London. Then on Monday the delegates resumed their discussions for a few more days before they wearily left for their homes. For Townshend, who always enjoyed synod sessions, it was back to the usual routine.

EXPANSION PROBLEMS WERE still a major issue for the Diocese of Huron. As has already been mentioned, Bishop Luxton was, from the outset of his episcopate, determined to build as many churches as were needed to serve the increasing attendance. Year after year in his annual report to Synod, he exhorted delegates to join him in this endeavour and induce their local congregations to subscribe liberally to this cause. By 1952 he exultantly reported that 25 new churches had been erected, along with halls and rectories.

However, two years later, this incredible growth began to slow down, much to Luxton's dismay. He tried hard to motivate his people to further action, but their response did not match his zeal. Part of the problem was the difficulty of maintaining enthusiasm for a cause over a number of years. Lethargy and lack of interest almost inevitably creep in following the initial flush of success. Moreover, Luxton seemed to think there was an unlimited supply of money available but, as Townshend knew, this was not the case.

When the flow of funds began to dwindle, the diocese resorted to two measures, one of which ultimately raised considerable concern. A special type of fund, known as the Revolving Fund, was created. Using a recent bequest for its original funds, Synod decided to raise 500,000 dollars as the amount required to make it workable. What was novel about the scheme was the manner in which the money was to be disbursed. A new congregation applying for a loan had to fulfill certain specific conditions. Architectural plans for the structure and a firm bid from a contractor had to be obtained. Then a detailed scheme explaining how the entire cost was going to be financed was submitted to the diocesan officials. Only then would the diocese extend a loan, but it was never to be large enough to cover the whole cost. The congregation was expected to repay ten per cent of the loan each year, together with annual interest payments of one per cent a year. This was a very low-cost system compared to the rates charged by the commercial banks, and certainly made it easier for new congregations to erect their buildings early.

The other method adopted to expedite the extension programme was not as financially sound nor as successful as the Revolving Loan Fund. Luxton decided to use bank overdrafts, which could be covered by the diocese's reserve funds if necessary. This scheme, in effect, was a form of deficit financing which even in the prosperous period of the 1950s was not a particularly wise procedure, and it was to cause Townshend much heartache.

Luxton's ambitions placed an enormous strain on the Church's resources. By 1951 the overdraft was 40,000 dollars.[52] A crisis had been reached! Luxton, Townshend and the Diocesan Commissioner, Archdeacon J.H.N. Mills, had to use all of their powers of persuasion to obtain sufficient contributions to offset this debt. Yet, in spite of the near catastrophe, Luxton was determined to continue using the overdraft method. In fact, it was retained, with many misgivings, for another four years, until a another system was devised and placed under Townshend's direction.

The Diocese of Huron was not the only part of the National Church facing financial difficulties. The activities of General Synod were becoming hampered by its limited financial resources. The National Church, which had never possessed extensive wealth, derived most of its funding from the laity. Its extensive commitment to support many missionary dioceses in the west and the north made it difficult to set aside funds for other programmes. General Synod assessed each diocese a certain sum, a method that had never been very successful as there was no compulsion for the diocese to contribute the required amount.

In the early 1950s, General Synod, as we have seen, decided to revamp its financial organization, and Townshend was one of the main experts drafted to help formulate a new approach. Calling on his experience in Huron, Townshend wanted the national body to adopt the apportionment scheme. A diocese was to be given a figure which they were required by canon law to raise and contribute. The resort to a canon-law requirement put teeth into this scheme. However, trying to persuade 28 dioceses to accept the plan was a monumental task, especially since General Synod did not possess any type of coercive power.

Townshend, and other champions of the apportionment plan, particularly the Rt. Rev. R.H. Waterman, Bishop of Nova Scotia, kept a steady stream of pressure on the separate dioceses. Gradually most of them fell into line. Many synods, including Huron, were not keen about being asked to donate higher amounts to the National Church when they needed the funds for their own projects. Consequently, Townshend became involved in negotiating and haggling with various officials in other dioceses about this plan.

On behalf of this scheme National Church offered to undertake deputation work; this meant travelling to other dioceses and speaking to their synods about the benefits. Townshend had used this technique in the 1940s when he was trying to improve givings in Huron; now he would utilize this device on the national scene. In 1954 he toured dioceses in the Prairie provinces and in British Columbia, explaining the needs of General Synod and extolling the advantages of the apportionment plan. One of the dioceses he was scheduled to visit was the Kootenay, located in the interior of British Columbia. At the moment, this see was vacant. Bishop Waterman thought it might be a good idea if Townshend were in the vicinity when the diocesan synod met to choose its new bishop. He hoped that Townshend might become a candidate.[53] Although he was not elected, it was, in fact, not the first time that his name had been considered for the episcopal office. Aside from this incident, his trip through the West was reasonably successful in achieving the aim of getting more dioceses to accept the new form of financing General Synod.

Another aspect of the National Church's life with which he was deeply involved was the work of the M.S.C.C. This arm of General Synod co-ordinated the Church's extensive missionary activity both at home among the native peoples and overseas, especially in China and Japan. These endeavours consumed large amounts of money, so once again Townshend's talents were enlisted. In the early fifties, he was a member of the financial committee of the M.S.C.C., often chairing it, and at the same time headed the sub-committee on Canadian missions. Unfortunately, the sparseness of the minutes fail to disclose the intense amount of time and labour these activities exacted from him, though we can be sure that he did not stint himself. Townshend had a reputation for getting through a committee's agenda rapidly, and he expected others to maintain the same pace as he did. If he had a meeting in Toronto, he rarely missed the train back home, even if it was the last one to leave Union Station.

Obviously, this work brought him considerable attention and, as noted above, his name was suggested for various bishoprics. Yet at no time did he ever really contemplate leaving his beloved Huron. He was a Huron man to the marrow of his bones. Since his own diocesan was a relatively young man, presumably any chance he had of succeeding to this see was remote. However, by 1955 Luxton was finding the responsibilities of his position very tiring. The confirmation tours alone were a serious drain on his energy. In 1955 he requested Synod to choose a suffragan bishop to assist him.

Normally in the Anglican Church a suffragan bishop is allotted a specific area within a diocese as his sphere of work. This region virtually becomes an independent unit, although the diocesan retains ultimate control over all of the suffragan's activities. However, Luxton did not envisage dividing the diocese. He simply wanted someone to help with confirmations and, as he added in his address to Synod, to assume the leadership of the flagging extension programme. Synod readily acceded to this request.[54]

An electoral synod was convened on September 19, 1955. Actually, the choice was virtually a foregone conclusion. Townshend was elected on the second ballot by a large majority of both the clerical and lay vote. It was a very moving moment for him. He had reached the pinnacle of success in his Church at the age of 57. After the applause died out when the vote was announced, he told Synod,

> I am overwhelmed, yet honoured by this expression of your confidence in me. This expression has made me feel very humble—and frightened. I cannot interpret your action, however, in any other way but that it is a new call from God to serve the church. I know I won't be alone but I shall need your prayers.[55]

Why was he elected suffragan bishop easily in 1955 after he had been denied the diocesan office seven years earlier? Church people might respond that it was the will of the Holy Spirit. Another explanation might say that Townshend was regarded as a good second man, one who could be relied upon to solve problems and get tasks performed. This was his strength. It may also have been a weakness. Some of his actions, especially in regard to raising funds, had often antagonized people. Many felt he only attended deanery meetings to discuss the budget or the need for more funds. His name was constantly linked with money. Rarely was he seen to be engaged in spiritual affairs. This accusation, while not entirely unmerited, was unfair. Luxton, on the other hand, with his masterly command of the English language, was seen as a man who could articulate a vision of the Church's role and purpose in a way that Townshend could not, even though many became weary of Luxton's idealism in a few years. Luxton used language in a way that lifted people above the blandness of daily routines, while Townshend's sermons and speeches usually dealt with mundane affairs. He gave homely advice drawn from his life and experiences as a farmer and a pastor. He did not paint glowing word pictures as Luxton did. In sum, Luxton appeared to be a gifted leader, and many laymen were attracted to his style.

Notwithstanding the earlier disappointment, the family was now ecstatic. Kathleen, that strong woman who had stood beside him all these years, was overjoyed at his elevation. The children were proud of their father and his accomplishments. There was much to do before the service of consecration scheduled for November 30, the Feast of St. Andrew the Apostle. One of the first things Townshend had to do was order episcopal regalia. He happily read the catalogues of the old English firm of J. Whippell & Co. Ltd. of Exeter to decide upon the proper shade of purple for his cassock, the length of his lawn rochet and the red and black chimers, the size of the purple shirts for daily attire, and other necessities. The whole cost came to $255.89. The other parts of his regalia—the ring, the pectoral cross, the pastoral staff or crozier—were presented by various groups at the service.

When the great day arrived, all was in readiness. The cathedral was beautiful and prepared for the service, couched in the sonorous language of the *Book of Common Prayer*. Several of Townshend's brother bishops had arrived to participate, including the Bishop of Western New York who represented the Episcopal Church of the United States. The service was conducted by the Most Rev. W.L. Wright, Archbishop of Algoma and Metropolitan of Ontario. The sermon was preached by his old friend, the Rt. Rev. F.H. Wilkinson, Bishop of Toronto. After Townshend was invested with his regalia, he imparted his first episcopal blessing to his people. It was a joyous event. What could mar it?

Actually, Townshend's health had almost ruined the day. For some time now he had been suffering from a very painful attack of lumbago in one of his legs. At times, he could hardly stand, and the consecration service usually lasted for two hours. He had been receiving treatments for this condition, and early in the morning before the service he received an extra one to help get him through the day. At any rate, he managed the service and the ensuing banquet at the old Hotel London, which was attended by over 500 people. He was now launched on his career as bishop.

CHAPTER FIVE

The Episcopate

Townshend was quickly caught up in his new episcopal duties. Bishop Luxton and his wife departed on a six-month sabbatical in Europe shortly after the consecration service, leaving Townshend in charge of the diocese. An intriguing series of letters crossed the Atlantic, revealing many of the problems facing diocesan leadership.[1] Securing new rectors for vacant parishes, matching the right clergyman with a congregation, negotiating stipends and living accommodations—these were just some of the problems about which the two men exchanged confidences. The tone of the letters was cordial, with Luxton constantly asking about Townshend's health, which had deteriorated since his consecration. Not only did he continue to suffer pains in his leg from the lumbago, but now he had been diagnosed as having diabetes, a condition that would afflict him for the rest of his life and that made some of his years in the active episcopate very trying.

With Luxton away in December of 1955, it fell to Townshend to compose the bishop's annual Christmas pastoral letter. This was the only such document Townshend ever penned. Writing in his homely, down-to-earth style, Townshend reiterated the traditional beliefs about Christmas, stressing that the Incarnation was the pivotal event in world history.

> Christ has done more to bless society and promote brotherhood than any other force in the world. Think of what influence, nameless and appealing, lay sleeping in that Manger; an influence that was to uplift the spiritual and moral life of this old world: [sic] From that Bethlehem Manger there shone a light that can never fail, revealing the spirit of God and softening the heart of this world, and making forever sacred the Mother and the Babe.[2]

This was a message ordinary Christians could understand and take to heart.

One of the new episcopal responsibilities which he thoroughly enjoyed was administering the Rite of Confirmation. Normally, in those years, confirmation candidates were 12 or 13 years old, although there were always a few adults who received this sacrament. Townshend loved travelling to parishes, especially rural ones, to conduct this service and deliver one of his fatherly sermons challenging young and old alike to cherish their new status in the Church and to continue to grow in their Christian faith.

His correspondence for these years contains dozens of letters to parish priests advising them on how he wished the confirmation service to be conducted. Huron's two bishops followed the *Prayer Book* liturgy without any deviations. Quite often he told rectors which hymns might be appropriate, and almost without exception he asked that his favourite one, "Breathe on Me Breath of God", be sung while the candidates were kneeling in front of him before he laid his hands on them.[3] After returning to London, he often dropped the rectors a note thanking them for the manner in which the service was conducted. If his pastoral staff was carried by a server, he would write the boy a letter commending him for the way in which it had been done. Townshend had the common touch, and rarely neglected an opportunity to express his appreciation of the effort put forth by ordinary people.

The joy which he derived from this service was not one-sided. Many Anglicans remember the day of their confirmation with fondness for years afterwards. One older person whom he confirmed, and who later became a priest, wrote,

> When I was confirmed at the age of 51, he was the officient. Our eyes met and his were smiling, all the way down to his heart. From that moment our relationship was one of quiet warmth and assurance. As the years passed, this part of his character and his function in the Church have deepened, ripened and become richer. He is a true father-in-God to all of us.[4]

During his visit to a parish, he always inquired about the rector's family. One priest noted, "Being a family man, he was much concerned with the welfare of the Rectory [sic] family, and especially I think in the case of the younger clergy to whom he must have been an inspiration."[5] One of these younger clerics, whose wife had just given birth to a baby boy, received a letter from Townshend thanking the young couple for letting him "come over to the house for coffee and to have a look at your new son."[6] Another rector wrote, "Whenever Bishop Townshend visited in our rectory over the years, he would take our children upon his knees to tell them the story of his pectoral cross and gold chain, letting them hold it in their little hands. He learned their names and to this day he asks about them by name."[7] Even after he retired, Townshend continued to take confirmations, and still provoked this same type of affectionate response.

There was more to being a bishop, however, than simply conducting confirmations and occasionally participating in the ordination of deacons and priests. There were new administrative duties. While he had to relinquish his many diocesan committee assignments as canon law required, he remained an *ex officio* member of the executive committee, from which he was able to wield considerable influence. He automatically became a member of the national House of Bishops but, at the same time, he retained his membership in some of the more important General Synod committees, especially the budget committee and the M.S.C.C. To these he added other duties. Through the efforts of his old friend, Rev. Maxwell Parker, head of the Anglican Book Centre, Townshend became vice-chairman under the primate of the Department of Information and Supplies. This role certainly enhanced his status in the inner workings of the National Church's administrative apparatus.[8]

While these appointments were significant, it was the diocesan area which had the first call on his time. Immediately after becoming suffragan bishop, he had been placed in charge of the Church Extension Committee's (C.E.C.) efforts, which, as previously indicated, had been flagging of late. Townshend instantly seized the nettle. The primary difficulty here was satisfying Bishop Luxton's inordinate demands for building more churches as quickly as possible. Townshend's more cautious approach soon became a major source of irritation between them.

In his first address to Synod in 1956 on this topic, the Suffragan Bishop warned the delegates that "we must build Churches only in areas where the local conditions justify such building; where we are reasonably sure of a bright future for the new Mission."[9] He then placed before Synod his plans for implementing the 300,000-dollar fund-raising campaign that had been authorized by the previous Synod. With a few minor amendments, Synod adopted his proposals, implicitly accepting his "go-slow" philosophy.[10] However, this episode, as it turned out, was the calm before the storm.

His efforts during the first few months in the episcopate, together with his health problems, had drained much of his energy. At the beginning of July, Kathleen and he went up to Bayfield, where he had recently purchased the cottage that had belonged to his former mentor, the Rev. E.C. Jennings. Here for a few weeks amidst quiet and familiar surroundings, he regained some of his strength, spending leisurely days chatting with old friends and casting his experienced eye over the summer's crops and the state of the farm community.

WITHIN A YEAR, CHURCH extension became the centrepiece of a memorable row at Synod. "Slowdown in Anglican Extension Puzzles Bishop" was the startling headline which greeted readers of the *London Free Press* when they opened their papers on the evening of May 7, 1957. The sub-heading was even more eye-catching: "View Conflicts with Group's Report."[11] These few words captured the nub of a bitter dispute between Huron's two episcopal leaders. Luxton had obtained a copy of the C.E.C.'s report, written by Townshend, which called for a sweeping change in policy: assisting "in the development of recently established parishes"[12] rather than erecting more buildings must now become the thrust of the committee's activity. "We must recognize that the flood-tide of Church Extension is over, for the time being, at least,"[13] was the committee's blunt assessment. It was that sentence, and its implications, which provoked the wrath that Luxton vented against his suffragan in the public forum of the Synod and that caused Townshend considerable emotional pain.

In his charge to the delegates at the opening of Synod, Luxton lashed out against the committee's recommendation. If other denominations, especially the Roman Catholic and the Gospel Hall, were still building churches, then the Anglicans must maintain their efforts. South-west Ontario, he claimed, was about to receive another influx of immigrants. Consequently, more churches were needed. Besides, he continued, the first stages of building a new church were relatively cheap and the local opposition to these projects should not be a deterrent.[14] His reference to a new wave of immigration was not completely accurate. As the C.E.C. pointed out, only a small portion of these people were Anglicans. Furthermore, the recently increased credit restrictions, the report argued, had had an adverse impact on the construction of new homes and other ventures.

The stage was set for a very heated clash. Townshend presented his commission's report, which boldly stated that a new church should be erected only "if it appears that there is any real future for it."[15] This criterion must now become the committee's guiding principle. Finally, the commission presented a series of resolutions, the most significant of which called for granting new parishes long-term loans rather than outright grants. The commission anticipated that this move would augment the resources of the Revolving Loan Fund and provide ready money when new buildings were really needed.

Luxton disliked all of these proposals, and bluntly said so! Immediately after Townshend finished speaking, an acrimonious debate erupted between the two men and their respective supporters. Unfortunately, the sparse records of the *Synod Journal* fail to capture the heat of the conflict. In the end, Synod endorsed the commission's report, an act which Townshend interpreted as a vindication of his policy. He was gratified by this support, telling one rector, "The Synod endorsement of the Church Extension Commission's work is a great support to me during the strain and stress of the sessions."[16] This episode aggravated the state of "cordial animosity" which one observer claimed existed between the two leaders.[17]

Still, the year was not all stress and strain. There were several moments that brought great happiness to Townshend and his wife. In January of 1957, they had travelled to Fredericton, N.B. for the consecration of his old friend, Henry O'Neil, as Bishop of Fredericton. Townshend presented O'Neil with his episcopal ring on behalf of the

Huron College Alumni.[18] In June the couple journeyed to New York City to help celebrate the 25th anniversary of one of his former student assistants, the Rev. T.J. Finlay. Townshend preached the sermon at the service in St. Bartholomew's Church, Park Avenue, where Finlay was the rector. The Townshends spent a glorious weekend at the Waldorf-Astoria Hotel, and were grandly entertained by the Finlays and members of the parish. For a couple who had never ventured very far beyond London together, it was an exciting trip, the subject of much conversation for weeks afterwards.[19]

A third episode that year which gave Townshend much pleasure was his acceptance of the Lamp of Learning Award from the O.S.S.T.F. The Federation wished to honour him for his support of improved salaries and benefits for teachers. Surprised at being granted this honour, he amusingly told an old friend, "I have said my greatest contribution to Education [sic] was to have married a school teacher, and together with her, having raised ten children, six of whom are in the teaching profession."[20]

This family was still growing, with the addition now of grandchildren. Gatherings on the great Christian festivals were moments of intense joy, as were the vacations at Bayfield with many of his children and their brood. Townshend was certainly not contemplating retirement, but time was passing, and he had reached that stage in life when many of his old colleagues and friends were either retiring or receiving their home-calls. While at the cottage that summer, he took a nostalgic trip down memory lane in a letter to a childhood friend, Louis MacKay, who was now living in Berkeley, California. In a long rambling epistle he recounted for his chum the activities, successes and situations of many of their former classmates, who were now widely scattered. "I just wish that we could get together to have a real, old-fashioned chin-wag. There is so much to be said. Looking back, we see some surprises. It is amazing to discover how far some of the students whom our teachers thought were pretty dull, have gone."[21] The yesteryears were beginning to take on a romantic glow as they receded further into the past.

HIS INTEREST IN THE CAUSE of education had not yet begun to wane. Among his many activities in this area was membership on the senate of the University of Western Ontario. He attended its meetings with the same degree of regularity as he did other organizations. By 1956, enrollment in the university was steadily increasing, and the only college on campus (other than the affiliates of Huron and Brescia Colleges), University College, was unable to accommodate the growing student body. A combined committee of the Board of Governors and the senate under the chairmanship of Prof. A.B. Conron was appointed to pursue the idea of opening another college. Townshend was one of the senate's representatives, but as the records show he was a very infrequent attender,[22] and took little part in the discussions except for the occasion when he stressed to the members the urgent need for another college to accommodate the increasing number of students.[23] Townshend had no connection with the new entity, named Middlesex College, after it was opened. His primary concern in senate meetings was to protect or extend the interests of Huron College.

It was the local Board of Education that remained at the centre of his educational interests. Although he declined the chairmanship in 1956, owing to his poor health and his new episcopal duties, he did accept the position two years later. His colleagues and he still faced the same problems they had all during this decade—the need for more schools and teachers, and the search for more funding as costs increased and as salaries and benefits continued to mount. The trustees felt they were constantly scrambling just to keep abreast of these demands. There seemed to be no end in sight. So it was these items which he reviewed in his valedictory speech that year.[24] It was simply a catalogue of worries facing the board.

Yet he did propose a novel idea, one he had been mulling over for some time. He wanted next year's board to open a summer school, in both the elementary and secondary panels, for students who failed to be promoted because "they are not quite ready for promotion, often through no fault of their own or their teachers. They are marginal cases who just cannot accomplish a full year's work in the school year. They might be able to accomplish a year's work in eleven months."[25] Here was a challenge for the new board. At first the Department of Education opposed the scheme, but within a few years the idea was adopted and put into practice. Townshend was not alone in pursuing this suggestion. He received support from other quarters. The Number 2 School Board of Yarmouth Township, near London, sent him a copy of their resolution endorsing his proposal.[26]

SCHOOL AFFAIRS WERE LEFT aside during the summer, as Townshend and Kathleen travelled to England to attend the Lambeth Conference of Anglican bishops. Beginning in 1867, the bishops of the Anglican Communion have met every ten years (except during the two world wars) at Lambeth Palace, the London residence of the Archbishop of Canterbury, to discuss major theological and social issues facing the world-wide Church. At the end of each conference the bishops issue a pastoral letter and a lengthy report with a series of resolutions about these problems. Given the dispersed mode of authority practised in the Anglican Communion, these pronouncements are usually accepted as guidelines for action rather than binding decrees.

Generally speaking, only diocesan bishops are invited to attend these meetings. Suffragan bishops are not present unless they have some special expertise which Canterbury wishes to use. By the time Townshend had been consecrated, invitations for the forthcoming conference had been extended, and as a suffragan he was not eligible. Naturally, he was eager to go, but Bishop Luxton had been unable to persuade Archbishop Fisher to extend an invitation to Townshend.[27] Undaunted, Townshend asked the Canadian Primate, Archbishop Barfoot, to intercede. Townshend stressed that his many, many services on behalf of the Canadian Church had earned him this privilege.[28] This bold bid paid off, for in February he received his official invitation to be one of the Lambeth fathers.[29]

Overjoyed, Kathleen and he could hardly wait to get on that boat for England. After the May sessions of the Huron Synod ended, they began to make their plans. Late in June, with their friends the O'Neils of Fredericton, and other Canadian episcopal families, they sailed from Montreal on one of the Canadian Pacific Steamship's Empress passenger liners.[30] After seven days, they arrived in Liverpool, took the boat-train to London, and registered at the Bonnington Hotel.

What thoughts must have passed through his mind as he stepped off the train and set foot in the city that was still for him the heart of the British Empire! Here was the boy from Huron County gazing at those sights he had seen countless times in photographs, newsreels and television programmes. Here he was standing in the city of the monarch, of the Houses of Parliament, of Westminster Abbey, and of the other St. Paul's Cathedral. No doubt these sights stirred vivid memories of the events and episodes he had studied in his British history courses many years ago at Huron College. It was both real and unreal. He was finally in the land of his ancestors, in the home of his beloved Church, and there was much to do and see.

Most important of all, of course, were the conference sessions. After the opening service in the ancient and magnificent Cathedral Church of Christ, Canterbury, the fathers got down to work. The usual procedure was to divide the bishops into working committees to consider each of the topics under review. Townshend was appointed to the committee on Progress in the Anglican Communion, whose chairman was the Rt. Rev. Walter Gray, Bishop of Connecticut, U.S.A. However, as the topic was very large, the parent committee was sub-divided into three units. Townshend was placed on the one dealing with Ministries and Manpower. The Bishop of Bath and Wells, England, the Rt. Rev. H.W. Bradfield, was its leader, and among its members was the Bishop of London, the Rt. Rev. H.C. Montgomery-Campbell and the Bishop of Southwell, the Rt. Rev. F.R. Barry, both well-known English prelates. Two Canadian members were Bishops Bagnell of Niagara and C.C. Robinson of Moosonee. Other bishops from around the world were also members, and soon a spirit of fellowship developed, which Townshend later claimed was one of the most important aspects of the conference for him. In later years he maintained a correspondence with some of these men.

This group was asked to survey the manpower needs of the whole communion, and to make recommendations for future development and deployment. Vocations to the ministry were declining by the end of the fifties, and the fathers strongly recommended that the Church seek new ways of involving the laity more extensively in ministry. This suggestion raised the question of the role of women in the Church, which was becoming a major issue. Sidestepping the controversial notion of ordaining women, the committee urged that Church leaders seek wider roles for women, especially for those who had been admitted to the order of deaconess. The committee also endorsed the growing practice of preparing older men for the priesthood, and noted that some dioceses already had special institutes for this purpose. Huron, for example, had recently opened Seager Hall, linked to the seminary at Huron College, for this purpose. Townshend described this move to his colleagues, and reference was made to it in the committee's final report. All in all, this document provided a thorough review of the Church's requirements for the next decade, and many of its recommendations were implemented by various national churches and provinces.[31]

It was not all work. Along with the service at St. Paul's Cathedral and the closing Eucharist at the Abbey, there were a number of social occasions. The Queen held a garden party at Buckingham Palace; various English ecclesiastical and political figures hosted receptions and dinners for the episcopal visitors and their wives. The Townshends enjoyed this whirlwind of entertainment, and even found time to visit the usual tourist sites.[32]

In late August, somewhat weary and slightly overwhelmed by it all but filled with happy memories, the Townshends and their friends boarded another of the Empress liners for home. Over the next few months, both bishops of Huron spoke to numerous groups about the conference, and cheerfully showed the slides they had taken. The best summary of Townshend's feelings about his participation came when he told a friend, "The Conference was the most moving, enriching and thrilling experience that I have had in my lifetime."[33]

RETURNING HOME MEANT picking up the old problems in the diocese and at the school board. Townshend kept a speaking engagement that fall which became a *cause célèbre*. In October, he delivered the keynote address at the annual meeting of the Public School Trustees Association of Ontario in Hamilton. While much of it was simply a recapitulation of the presidential address given to this same group some years earlier, it was his opening comments which created the furor.

Claiming that the public school system was the most important unifying force in the country, he went on to assert that,

> To my mind, the greatest miracle in this whole Public School system is that in spite of all religions, and no religion being represented, there is integrated into this whole organization the strong fibre of spiritual strength and an actual programme of religious instruction. The rights of the minority are protected in this question of religious instruction in the Public Schools but on the other hand, the rights of the large majority are also protected by being given religious instruction.[34]

This statement was innocent enough, but he went on scathingly to excoriate those whom he regarded as enemies of the system and who, in his opinion, were determined to wreck it. "There are those within this province who would destroy this system; who would throw it right out the window. These people are not confined to any one religious denomination. There are those who desire a completely dual system—Roman Catholic and Protestant."[35] Here was the crux of the matter. The Roman Catholics were again trying to obtain more financial support for their hard-pressed Separate Schools. Part of their strategy was to claim that their schools were public and deserved the same assistance as the regular public ones. Townshend regarded this allegation as utter nonsense. Separate Schools were just that—separate! How could they be a part of the public system if they restricted their clientele to the adherents of one denomination?

While Townshend had refrained from making direct references to the Roman Catholics in his speech, they had no doubts that they were the target. A few days later, the Diocesan Trustees Association of the Roman Catholic Diocese of London passed a resolution denying that Catholics had any intention of undermining the public school. Rather, they stated, they were proud of the system, and re-emphasized their argument that Separate Schools were members of it: "On the contrary, we are proud that legally the Separate Schools of this province are an integral part of the Public School system." They pledged to support all groups seeking solutions to the many complex problems facing boards of education around the province.[36]

Yet Townshend, the old anti-Catholic warhorse, was not duped by this polite phrasing. He warned the Rev. J.V. Mills, secretary of the Public Trustees Association, that this group must be constantly vigilant and speak out in clear terms on this matter.[37] As it turned out, the Roman Catholics were indeed about to launch a major campaign to secure more funding for their schools.

As this crowded year began to wind down, Townshend received another honour that touched him deeply. For the first time in its history, the London Board of Education named a new school after one of its sitting members. A new elementary school, located in Knollwood Park, was officially opened on the evening of December 10th, 1958, and called the Bishop Townshend Public School. Surrounded by family, fellow trustees and other well-wishers, he accepted an oil painting of himself, which he then, in turn, gave to the school. R.D. Schoales, the board's architect, presented him with a golden key to the building, after which F.W. Rivers, Deputy Minister of Education (and another of Townshend's cronies) gave the official address. At the end of the proceedings, Townshend imparted his blessing on the assembled group and the new school. A happy social hour followed. That evening remained a joyous event in his memory for the rest of his life.[38]

Shortly after, he was elected chairman of the board's Property Committee, a post he was to hold for the next several years. (This committee changed its name several times but its tasks were substantially the same.) In effect, he became the czar of the board's acquisitions and building projects. Certainly he was a fitting choice, considering his intimate acquaintance with real estate and construction.

TOWNSHEND CONTINUED TO exercise similar control over the diocese's construction programme, even though he and Bishop Luxton remained at odds on church extension. As head of the C.E.C., the Suffragan Bishop reported annually to Synod on its activities, noting the number of new buildings erected and sites purchased for future development. Money was again becoming a problem. By the end of the 1950s, the post-war boom was slowing down; interest rates were starting to climb; and unemployment was rising. It was becoming more difficult to secure adequate financing for construction. Donations to the C.E.C. began to decline. In fact, the campaign begun in 1956 to raise 300,000 dollars fell short of its objective by a considerable amount, although donations kept trickling in.

Consequently, the diocese resorted to other expedients. The former scheme of using overdrafts was revived, though Townshend was never very keen about using it. Older, wealthier parishes were encouraged to help subsidize newer ones. But this appeal had only a limited response. In reporting to Synod about church extension in these years, Townshend always tried to put the best possible face on the situation, but it was clear to all that growth was slowing down. In 1963, he told Synod that,

> It is obvious, therefore, that Church Extension in the Diocese of Huron must virtually come to a standstill for the time being. Whether it remains at a standstill or surges forward with renewed vigour is up to the Church people of this Diocese of Huron. It is up to us to show, with dollars and cents, whether we really are concerned about this Extension of the Church of Jesus Christ in the Diocese and beyond.[39]

Nevertheless, church extension continued, although to the annoyance of Luxton at a much slower pace. The Bishop was not about to surrender his cherished hope of seeing new churches rising everywhere in Huron.

By the early 1960s, the diocese's continued growth was creating problems for its administrative machinery. Its governing structure needed reorganizing. While its sheer geographical extent had always presented difficulties, the addition of six or seven new parishes each year placed tremendous strain on the two bishops. In 1959, Synod appointed a committee to study the future organization of the diocese and to make recommendations about the possibility of increasing the number of bishops. During the deliberations, the idea emerged of subdividing the diocese into three areas, each with its own suffragan bishop, who would exercise full episcopal functions in his area, subject to the overall authority of the diocesan bishop. This would mean electing another suffragan.[40]

This plan, if adopted, had serious and far-reaching consequences for Townshend. Did it mean that he had to move away from London to reside in another part of the diocese? Certainly the authors of the report anticipated such action. This was a delicate matter and, given the uneasy relations between Luxton and Townshend, it had to be negotiated very carefully. When the committee met with Townshend in January, 1960 to discuss this possibility, they offered him a compromise solution. He could retain his London residence but open an office in his area of jurisdiction.[41] He flatly rejected the proposal! Instead, he sharply criticized the scheme itself. Stating that he had been elected suffragan bishop of the whole diocese, not just a section of it, he retorted, "I have never asked for a change in those duties, and it is not my intention to do so." After living in London for 34 years, he had no desire to leave.

"Furthermore," he argued, "I do not think that this proposed 'pilot project' [sic] will work out satisfactorily. I feel that we should not experiment on the Episcopal level."[42] (Here he was being slightly disingenuous, for there was nothing new about using suffragans in this way.) Instead, he suggested that a new diocese be carved out of the existing one, an idea that had been mooted for years but had never seriously been contemplated. Even he seemed to be using it as a mere stalking-horse, for he went on to tell the group it was too early to attempt such a move. Perhaps he was just being pernickety. The diocese definitely needed more episcopal assistance.

Indeed, his tough stand left the committee with a dilemma. After considerable deliberation, it recommended that Townshend be left in his present situation and that another suffragan be chosen for the northern part of the diocese, which desperately required a bishop's oversight.[43] Synod readily adopted this suggestion.[44] Archdeacon Harold Appleyard of Brantford was elected as the second suffragan, assuming the title of Bishop of Georgian Bay. Townshend's deteriorating health was further undermined by the strain of this episode, which had continued for several months.

Some of this pain had been eased earlier when the University of Western Ontario bestowed upon him the honorary degree of Doctor of Laws (LL.D.) at its spring convocation in 1960.[45]

Coincidentally, it was the last time convocation was conducted outdoors in the J.W. Little Memorial Stadium. On that bright sunny day, June 5, 1960, together with his fellow honorary graduates—Greg Clark, the humorist and journalist; Arthur Ford, the editor of the *London Free Press*; and the Rev. Alexander Nimmo, a Presbyterian clergyman—he paraded down the hill to the field, received his honorary degree, and gave the benediction at the end of the ceremony.[46]

AS THE DECADE OF the fifties ended, hardly anyone realized that its successor would be so decidedly different. The sixties was one of those eras in which the forces of change virtually obliterate the lines of continuity with the past. It became a raucous period, which threw out serious challenges to many aspects of traditional society. Neither the churches nor educational institutions escaped the impact of the swift currents of change that engulfed North America and Western Europe. The major denominations suffered declining attendance and reduced contributions—a reversal of the previous 15 years. Equally serious for church people were the increasing number of attacks directed against the basic tenets of the Christian faith. Christianity has always had critics, but in this decade many of the challenges came from within the ranks of Christian theologians, who used modern media to disseminate their opinions. Soon, Christians were hearing about "situational ethics", which, by and large, denied the reality of absolute values. Perhaps the greatest shock for the laity was talk about the "death of God". Leaders of this brand of theology were explicitly trying to redefine the traditional conception of God. Both of these challenges, and others, were extremely disturbing to the ordinary churchgoer, even though such ideas had been circulating among academic scholars for decades.[47]

For education it was an equally upsetting decade. In Ontario the public and separate systems not only continued to expand physically, as they had been doing for 15 years, but they underwent the most sweeping reforms since public education had been established in the previous century. Reform was the order of the day everywhere in the Ontario public school system but particularly, as will be recounted, in the secondary schools. By the end of the decade one could hardly recognize the old and venerable Ontario collegiate institute. Trying to accommodate the huge influx of students at this level and to supply Ontario's manpower demands, the government developed a new type of high school that had a more flexible curriculum and less stringent graduation requirements. It was a secondary system designed to meet the needs of both a different kind of student and a different society.[48]

Inevitably Townshend became involved in many of these developments, though he often expressed mixed feelings about them. Some he applauded, while others provoked dismay and even suspicion in his mind about their origins and ultimate effect. Perhaps what was not clearly apparent to him was that the world in which he had been raised and worked was passing away, and that tremendous readjustments were required to fit into the different kind of society that was beginning to emerge. But he was certainly not alone in this regard.

Along with the challenges emerging in the ecclesiastical and educational worlds, these years also brought many unsettling episodes in Townshend's personal life. The first occurred in January, 1961, when he assumed a new position he certainly had not sought and did not relish undertaking. When the principal of Huron College, the Rev. Michael Coleman, was elected Bishop of Kootenay, the College Council asked Townshend to become the acting principal. With great reluctance, coupled with his inability to refuse responsibility, Townshend added this heavy administrative chore to his already overburdened schedule. As he told one of his old clerical friends, "Making me the Acting Principal was a crazy idea, because I have already more work than I can do properly. I am pressing for the appointment of a Principal."[49] He pushed the council hard to find a replacement.

So, for a few months he had to deal with the multitude of problems which beset the head of a college—hiring faculty, negotiating salaries, raising funds. Since he was able to spend only a few hours a week at this job, he was fortunate to have the assistance of two very able academic administrators, the Rev. J.G. Rowe, Dean of Arts and the Rev. John Grant Morden, the Registrar. Morden, as it turned out, was Townshend's candidate for the principalship.

During his short tenure, Townshend did preside over one happy event in the college's life, the annual convocation. As principal he presented four distinguished churchmen to the Chancellor of the University of Western Ontario for honorary degrees. These were the Very Rev. William Sewell, Dean of Regina; Archdeacon Cameron

Queen, the Diocesan Commissioner; the Rev. Canon A. Brant Thomas; and the Rt. Rev. Michael Coleman, the Bishop of Kootenay and formerly the head of Huron College. At the end of May, Townshend eagerly handed over his duties to Dr. Morden, who first became vice-principal and then in a few months ascended to the principalship.

WHILE HE WAS RELIEVED of this educational task, another and far more onerous matter was looming. London City Council had finally decided to carry out its major annexation scheme. On January 1, 1961 London acquired those large blocks of land to the east of the city that it had long been coveting. London's physical boundaries leapt from 32.03 square kilometres to 171.898 square kilometres. By a stroke of the pen, its population rose from 63,072 to 165,815.[50] This phenomenal growth added an enormous number of elementary and secondary schools—together with thousands of students, teachers, and support staff—to London's already burgeoning system.

Who would want to be chairman of the school board in this situation? That was Townshend's fate (or good luck) in 1962. For the sixth, and the last, time he was elected to this post.[51] The issues surrounding the annexation episode, especially the financial ones, became the centrepiece of his last inaugural address.[52] He warned his fellow trustees that it was going to be difficult to follow their "pay as you go policy" and to use short-term debentures to ease their financial burden. These instruments would probably not be sufficient to handle the large debt of 546,948 dollars that had been inherited from the small boards. Increasing the property tax, Townshend reasoned, was the only way to discharge this large sum. Raising taxes, however, is always an unpopular move. To add to this difficulty, an outcry was heard in the city against what some citizens were calling "gold plated" schools. In an attempt to allay this discontent, the chairman quoted statistics to show that the cost of school construction locally was well below the provincial average.[53] Ultimately, the trustees were forced to raise the property rate, but even so the debt was not eliminated, and continued to bedevil board business not only for the rest of 1962 but for many years afterward.

Townshend also argued that the increased responsibilities which annexation had brought necessitated an extensive reorganization of the board's bureaucracy. In particular, he sought the appointment of a Superintendent of Special Education and Professional Services. This new functionary could relieve the Superintendent of Public Schools of many of his administrative chores. Townshend further cajoled the trustees into beginning the search for quarters to house all the administrators. This was an urgent need. Presently these people were scattered around the city in a number of buildings, which made communicating awkward. At the end of his address, Townshend seized the opportunity to do a little sermonizing on the real role of a trustee, that of providing a proper education for all of London's children.

> All of these policies are related to our aim of providing opportunities for the "good life" in all the varied aspects of the meaning of this term, to those for whom we have committed ourselves when we accepted trusteeship on this Board. Concern for the educational well-being of our boys and girls must ever come first.[54]

The board immediately set about responding to this challenge. The next 12 months proved to be extremely busy ones as the trustees tried to solve the problems created by annexation and, at the same time, keep pace with the burgeoning school population. Two more high schools were added to the city's system in 1962, while extensions were built onto many secondary and elementary buildings. The board remodeled its administrative component as Townshend had suggested. W.D. Sutton was appointed as the new Director of Education; J.D. Given became Superintendent of Public Schools; and M.W. Chalmers was selected as the first Superintendent of Special Education. A new Inspector of Public Schools was also appointed. The successful candidate was Townshend's son, John, then principal of an elementary school. This choice, as with other appointments his relatives and *protégés* received, provoked charges of nepotism. This is a difficult allegation to prove as there is no documentary evidence available, but there is little doubt that Townshend always looked after the interests of his family.

The trustees also found a new home for the board's offices as the chairman had requested. The old London Normal School became vacant that year when this institution moved into new quarters, Elborn College, close to the university. The splendid nineteenth-century building would suit the administrators very well. A lease was obtained on the old building, and for more than two decades it became the centre of London's public education system.

Like so many boards around the province in those years, London's was constantly hiring more teachers. This need became particularly acute as more of the baby-boom generation entered secondary school. At that time there was only one training institution for teachers at this level, the Ontario College of Education, located in Toronto. In 1956 the Department of Education had initiated a temporary summer course to prepare secondary teachers. Under this scheme a board hired recent university graduates who then took their professional training during two summers. After the first summer session and with very inadequate practice teaching, these beginners were summarily dumped into the classrooms.

Referring to this practice, Townshend warned the board "that the proportion of inexperienced teachers in our schools continues to increase."[55] In 1962 virtually one-third of the secondary teachers London hired were products of the emergency summer course. "This situation," he underlined, "emphasizes the need for adequate supervision and in-service training."[56] However, since this problem obviously was going to last for several years, more Colleges of Education were needed. London added its voice to the growing chorus of complaints about this situation. Finally, the provincial government announced that two more colleges were going to be built. Townshend happily informed the board at the end of the year that "one of the centres will be London."[57]

WHILE THE INFLUX OF students had increased the need for more teachers, the introduction of a new programme of studies for secondary schools, known as the Reorganized Programme (sometimes called the Robarts Plan after the Minister of Education), was an equally important factor. This scheme dramatically revised the purposes and structure of secondary education in Ontario. The initial impulse for this series of revisions came from outside Ontario. At the beginning of the decade the Canadian economy was experiencing a recession. Part of the cause, it was argued, was Canada's lack of a sufficient supply of trained skilled workers. Furthermore, it was argued, Canada did not have enough facilities to train such people. As a way of alleviating this situation, the Diefenbaker government decided to offer financial assistance to any province that desired to improve its vocational-training institutions. In 1960 Parliament enacted the Technical and Vocational Training Assistance Act, which enabled the federal government to pay 75 per cent of these expenditures for three years—with the stipulation that the money was to be used solely for constructing or enlarging provincially-owned institutions. At the time, Ontario had very few of these, and the Department of Public Works claimed that it did not have the capacity to build a sufficient number in the three years during which Ontario could take advantage of the federal government's largesse. Potentially, then, Ontario, the industrial heart of the nation, might have lost out on this programme. In a rather bold move, the Ontario cabinet pressured its federal counterpart to permit it to use the funding to build *vocational schools* on the local level. Thus it was the local boards in Ontario, and not the provincial government, which directly benefited from this scheme. In the next few years, hundreds of new vocational schools were erected and technical wings added to already existing collegiate institutes.

Once the government had decided to expand the facilities for technical training, it became obvious that an entirely new high-school programme was needed. The existing one, based on a limited academic base, was not sufficient for the demands of the new economy. Within a very short period of time, the Department of Education produced a radically revised programme of studies for all potential high-school students. The programme established three five-year tracks or branches, each of which was to lead to Grade 13 and to give students entrance to university. The first track, named the Arts and Science Programme, was simply a revamping of the traditional academic fare. The other two tracks were labelled Business and Commerce, and Science, Technology and Trades. While these latter branches were to emphasize the areas contained in their titles, in reality the traditional academic subjects continued to take precedence despite the fact that it was a major assumption of this scheme that the three university-bound tracks would have equal status. In other words, the Department was attempting to persuade the public, and particularly parents, that business and technical subjects were equivalent to academic ones.

The really new and innovative part of the Reorganized Programme, however, was the creation of a parallel set of four-year tracks, ending in Grade 12. The same names were applied to the three branches (Arts and Science; Business and Commerce; Science, Technology and Trades), but they were designed for a different type of student—one with average ability. Preparation for immediate entry into the work world at the end of high school was the objective of the "Four-Year Programme". (Up to this point post-secondary education in Ontario had remained closed to such students.) Moreover, the courses in this programme were not to be watered-down versions of their "academic" counterparts but were to be *relevant* and *practical*, in keeping with the needs of this group of adolescents. (As it turned out, many innovative and exciting courses were devised for this level, but ironically they contributed to the early demise of the whole Reorganized Programme.) Finally, a two-year Occupational course was established for students of low ability. This stream concentrated on instilling practical skills to prepare these youths for immediate job placement.[58]

There is no doubt that the Reorganized Programme met with acclaim. It certainly enhanced the adolescent's opportunity to receive technical education at the secondary level. Almost overnight the Ontario Collegiate Institute, known far and wide for its academic excellence, was transformed into a different kind of secondary institution. From being a somewhat elitist type of training ground, it soon became a school for the masses, catering to a wide diversity of young people possessing a multitude of abilities and interests. Attendance and retention rates soared, while the number of students who dropped out of high school significantly declined for a number of years.

How did this new programme accord with Townshend's long-standing interest in vocational education? Actually, many of its elements appeared in the London Board's submission to the Hope Commission a decade-and-a-half earlier. As we have seen, Townshend had constantly called for an upgrading of the vocational stream to make it as socially respectable as the academic one, just as the Robarts Plan now attempted to do. Many of the new courses designed for the four- and two-year streams incorporated the practical bent which he had strenuously advocated for this type of student. In many, many ways the Reorganized Programme fulfilled his desire for a more useful secondary-school system.

Unhappily for Townshend's expectations, the new scheme remained in existence for only a few years. Very early it began to fall apart, partly owing to forces outside the educational system and partly to weaknesses within the scheme itself.[59] The four-year tracks, for which there had been such great expectations, proved to be a disappointment. Many of the courses, despite the Department's admonitions, were merely carbon copies of the five-year ones, and did not offer a fresh approach for the average student. Often, students who were discipline problems or who were not succeeding in the five-year tracks were summarily shunted into a four-year stream. But the real problem with the latter programme was that the students had no place to go, after Grade 12, to receive additional training. Before the introduction of the Colleges of Applied Arts and Technology in 1966, these graduates were simply dumped onto the job market, which, at that moment, could not absorb so many semi-skilled people. Also, some of the really innovative courses that were developed in the four-year streams became attractive to students and teachers in the five-year branches, and they wanted to try some of these different ideas. Towards the end of the decade the Department of Education permitted a few chosen high schools to design very flexible timetables for the entire student body. But after a short flourish the Reorganized Programme died. Although Townshend did not make any public statement lamenting its demise, he was not impressed with what succeeded it.

IN HIS 1962 INAUGURAL address the new chairman referred to the introduction of the new approach in Grade 9, and informed trustees that board officials had been explaining it to parents, students, businessmen and teachers. Townshend wryly added, "There is still much to be done in informing the public fully about the new programmes."[60] No doubt there was! As he well realized, many parents still wanted their children enrolled in the university-oriented course (Five-Year Arts and Sciences) rather than the vocational ones, which still had a stigma attached to them.

As proof of the existence of this attitude, he indicated that of the 1,744 London students enrolled in the five-year tracks, only 191 had opted for the Science, Technology and Trades strand and even fewer, 174, for the Business and Commerce programme. Obviously, the majority had chosen the Arts and Science strand, even though *all* five-year programmes led to university entrance. At the other extreme, 283 students had entered the Two-Year Occupations track, which prepared pupils for immediate entry into the work force. The response, in London at least, to the four-year programmes was minimal, although Townshend expected this track would become more popular in the future; and, in fact, it did.

The increased emphasis on the vocational aspect of secondary education also led to another innovation in London's secondary schools (as these institutions were now officially called).[61] Special vocational classes for older students were opened, financed by the federal government under the Technical and Vocational Training Assistance Act. These courses were given at night, and offered a wide range of technical subjects with a decidedly practical orientation. Townshend was delighted at this development, telling the board, "These classes are the first application of a new philosophy concerning public education—the necessity of training and retraining to meet the challenge of the new era."[62] He became a staunch advocate of what was soon being called lifelong education.

This strenuous year for the board finally came to a close. In thanking Townshend for his leadership during the past months, C.C. Carrothers called 1962 "perhaps the busiest year in London Board history."[63] He may well have been right. But, as if Townshend and his co-workers did not have enough to contend with on the local scene, another major educational issue—and an old one in Ontario history—reared its head towards the end of the year—the question of financing Roman Catholic Separate Schools. The Romans were on the march again! Once more Townshend and his various allies had to mount the barricades in defense of the public school system.

Growth and expansion had created severe problems for the Separate School boards, and they were hampered in trying to solve them by inadequate financial resources. By the beginning of this decade the Separate boards were in desperate straits, and might very well have been forced to close many or perhaps all of their schools.[64] In October, 1962 the Roman Catholic hierarchy submitted a lengthy brief to the cabinet requesting, among other things, the extension of their system to the end of Grade 13 and full funding for their schools, including a share of the industrial and commercial property tax, which was an extremely lucrative source of revenue.[65] These demands were potentially explosive for the government; moreover, they could not have been made at a more difficult moment. The Department of Education was currently attempting to devise a new method of awarding school grants. As the Tories well knew, extending more funding to the Roman Catholic schools was politically dangerous. Their Protestant and rural supporters would be reluctant to approve any concession to the Catholics.

Briefs and petitions poured into the government, denouncing the Catholic claims. One of these was submitted by the Anglican Provincial Synod and was signed by all of the bishops, including Townshend. This document was couched in more conciliatory language than Anglicans had often used in the past, but it still objected to giving increased grants to the Romans. While the Anglican bishops applauded the desire of the Roman Catholics to link religion and education, they feared that extending the separate system would only balkanize the public one.[66] A committee composed of Archbishop W.L. Wright of Algoma, Bishop F. Wilkinson and Suffragan Bishop H.R. Hunt (both of Toronto), and Townshend was chosen to meet with Premier Robarts on December 12, 1962 to discuss the Anglican submission. However, the only reaction these clerics seemed to have obtained at the meeting was a polite expression of gratitude for their attendance.[67] The *Globe and Mail* reported Premier Robarts as simply saying that he had "read the brief with great interest. As with other briefs I've received, this one will be examined very carefully." Hardly a rousing endorsement!

Even before his brother bishops had penned their mildly worded critique, Townshend had complained about the appearance of a more conciliatory attitude throughout the province towards the Roman Catholic requests. He told a fellow Orangeman,

> I have discovered a strong feeling upon the part of people in this Province that the children in the Roman Catholic schools must get equal treatment with the children of the Public Schools. I have a feeling that the benevolent attitude of Pope John who has looked upon all Church members as brothers, though "separated brethren", has influenced the thinking of our people. I certainly know that it has influenced the thinking of some of our Anglicans. They feel that they must be broad-minded and generous; but as some have said, we must ever be on guard lest our broad-mindedness is nothing more than shallow-mindedness.[68]

Townshend never denied that separate-school pupils were entitled to the same quality of education as their public-school counterparts. In his mind there was a very simple solution: "If the Roman Catholics desired to have the same quality of education they could obtain it by sending their children to the Public Schools."[69] This was hardly a reasonable resolution, and certainly disregarded much history and constitutional law. He also criticized the Catholics for describing their schools as part of the public system and for referring to the public schools as "Protestant Schools."[70]

Within a few months the government had devised a scheme which avoided another emotional public debate over this contentious issue. In February, 1963 the Minister of Education announced a new method of awarding grants to school boards. Part of this scheme was a series of equalization grants for boards which lacked the large tax base possessed by the wealthier communities in the southern parts of the province. In a deft political move, Separate Schools were included in the new arrangement. This action gave the Roman Catholic boards more funding, but did not grant them a share in the corporation property tax; nor did it extend the separate system to the end of high school. All parties achieved something by this deal but, as usual, not all groups, especially the Roman Catholic hierarchy, were satisfied. They had obtained more money, but their system remained truncated. And while they accepted the offer, they obviously would return to the field to do battle again.[71]

For Townshend, amidst these trying political struggles, one event that spring stood out. On Trinity Sunday, May 13, 1962, at the family's parish Church of the Redeemer, he ordained his son, Robert, as a deacon. Surrounded by the family and a host of friends, Townshend enjoyed one of those very rare occasions when a bishop can carry out this rite. He told one of his Goderich Township cronies, "Conducting the service of Ordination for my son was one of the most moving experiences of my life. It was a good Service, and Dr. John Morden (Principal of Huron College) preached the best Ordination sermon that I have ever heard."[72] Letters of congratulation poured in from a wide range of well-wishers, including the Most Rev. John Cody, Roman Catholic Bishop of London. A year later, Townshend raised Bob to the priesthood, and also conducted his wedding.[73]

AFTER A QUIET SUMMER, Townshend attended General Synod held in Kingston that fall. This convocation undoubtedly marked the high point of his service to the Canadian Church. It adopted a new pension scheme, the result of four years of intensive labour and many meetings of a small commission chaired by Townshend. General Synod had originally established a national pension scheme in 1921, but many dioceses, including Huron, had preferred to use their own plans. Successive revisions of the national one had gradually persuaded more dioceses to join it, including, as previously noted, Huron. By the middle of the fifties the changing economic conditions had dictated another review of the plan with the hope of attracting the non-member dioceses to subscribe to it. General Synod in 1955 requested the Primate to establish a special committee, composed of people not attached to the Pension Board, to investigate the pension plan. Two years later the Executive Council also asked the Primate to set up a committee to determine if Synod's request was feasible and to nominate members for the proposed commission. This committee reported that the task could be done, and suggested that the commission be limited to three people.[74]

Armed with this advice, Archbishop Barfoot approached Townshend to head up the commission. For the other two members he suggested P. DuMoulin of London and John Osler of Toronto.[75] At first Townshend was reluctant to take on a task which he feared was going to be onerous and consume much time. He claimed he lacked sufficient knowledge of the subject, which was either a statement of modesty or simply misleading, as he had been involved with pension matters in the diocese and at the London Board of Education for two decades. Placing a bishop at the head of the commission, he told the Primate, was wrong, although he did not give explicit reasons for this argument. He also felt it was improper to appoint the other members from the same area of the country. This might cause dissension in the rest of the Church. However, he agreed to accept the task if he were relieved of the chairmanship of the General Synod Committee on the Financial Needs of the Church and if the commission did not have to report to the upcoming General Synod sessions in 1959. There was not sufficient time, he felt, to accomplish this work before General Synod met. Also, he told the Primate that DuMoulin had declined to serve, and recommended J.H. (Jake) Moore, an executive with Labatt's Brewery in London, as a better choice than himself.[76] Barfoot readily agreed to the substitution of Moore for DuMoulin, but virtually demanded that Townshend be a member of the committee. So once again Townshend accepted another chairmanship.[77]

Over the next year and a half, these three men, assisted by Mr. Gordon Hamill, another executive from Labatt's, spent hours pouring over a variety of pension plans used by other dioceses, the Episcopal Church of the United States, and many other denominations, trying to devise a scheme that assured adequate pension benefits for retired clergy, their widows and children. Attempting to satisfy the divergent views of 28 dioceses, spread across regions of Canada with different economies, was a daunting task. Still, by early 1960 they had cobbled together a plan which Townshend described to Bishop Steer, chairman of the Pension Board, as one that "will be of great practical benefit to the clergy and their widows."[78] He also noted that they had adopted a clause to handle the special needs of priests who had been on minimum stipends, especially those who had spent most, if not all, of their working lives in the mission field.

Composing the plan was one thing; getting it adopted by the layers of the central administration and member dioceses was another. The first hurdle was the Pension Board. However, this group was delighted with the proposed scheme, and readily adopted it with a few minor revisions. Townshend's group did not object to these changes. Before presenting it to the House of Bishops, which was to meet in Oakville in August, Townshend, leaning on his well-honed political skills, suggested to Bishop Steer and the Primate that it might be wise to disclose the plan's terms to the non-participating dioceses. The improved benefits might persuade one or more of them to join it, and thus enhance its worth. No doubt he had his eye on Toronto—the wealthiest and most populous diocese in the country—which was still a holdout.[79] When the Toronto Synod voted late in May to enter the new national plan, Townshend was overjoyed. He heaped effusive praise on his old friend, Bishop Fred Wilkinson of Toronto, for his energetic leadership in the cause. It was the icing on the cake![80]

Thus the stage was set for Townshend to step before the House of Bishops on August 26, 1960 to introduce the plan. If it was accepted here, then passage through General Synod was virtually assured. Actually, it was Hammill who was tipped to explain its intricacies to the assembled prelates. Before introducing his colleague, Townshend laid the groundwork by emphasizing some of the plan's most important features. In particular, he noted that the benefits for all participants would be increased over the present scheme and that it was the commission's conviction "that future pension benefits should be based on the assessable salary rate of each Clergyman, and should not be a fixed benefit for all Clergymen."[81] This latter aspect was a decided change from the previous scheme, under which all contributors received approximately the same amount of pension regardless of number of years of service. The Townshend plan brought the Church's scheme into line with most contemporary secular ones. The subsequent discussion in the House revolved around the details, but no major challenges were offered, and it was easily adopted.

After receiving approval here, the plan reverted to the hands of the Pension Board, which had to compose a new canon law to embody the scheme before it could be submitted to the next General Synod. The explanation and defence of it at that meeting became the responsibility of the chairman of the Pension Board. After a lengthy debate on the floor of General Synod in Kingston in 1962, during which several amendments were introduced, the plan was adopted and subsequently went into operation.

Townshend, of course, was immensely pleased with the final result. Once again, he had been able to provide an adequate retirement allowance for a group who did not always receive a fair share of the world's rewards. It was another link in that long chain of salary and benefit improvements he had been striving to forge since he had entered public life in the 1930s.

HIS ELATION AT THIS triumph was tempered, however, by the disclosure that his diabetic condition had begun to affect his eyes, making it almost impossible for him to function. His doctors urged him to take time off to try to get the affliction under control. Resignedly he took a six-months leave from his episcopal duties, remaining inactive in an attempt to recuperate. But his condition became so serious that he was advised to permanently reduce his many activities, especially the incredible number of committees on which he served. With a heavy heart and great reluctance, Townshend resigned from all of his General Synod posts, including the chairmanship of the budget committee, which he had only assumed in the previous year. In a letter full of pathos he told Archbishop Clark, "This is a letter which I find difficult to write. In recent months I have been having great difficulty with a physical disability; so much so that I have come to the place where I feel that I must retire from my General Synod responsibilities."[82] Then he listed the various committees from which he was retiring; there were seven in all. Most were major ones, and on some of them he had served since 1939. It was a wrenching experience, but it had to be done. Certainly the time off helped to improve his health but, as it turned out, it was only a temporary reprieve. He was plagued by poor health for the next few years.

Yet, the entire year was not totally consumed by his health problems. In the spring Kathleen and he spent some more time at the Bayfield cottage, while in August they travelled to Toronto where he attended a few sessions of the Anglican Congress, a world-wide meeting of bishops, clergy and laity.[83] Officially Townshend was a delegate from the Diocese of Huron, but he took little part in the discussions. He simply was not up to it. Perhaps the most memorable aspect for him was renewing his friendship with episcopal colleagues whom he had met at the Lambeth Conference five years earlier. After a few days, he returned home for more rest.

The new year saw him back in harness. His health had improved, but he was warned not to take on too much. Never one to shun responsibility and finding it difficult to remain inactive, he assumed the chairmanship of the Board of Education's property committee. Once more he was thrust right into the centre of the on-going acquisition problem. The city's growing population was rapidly pushing out into the suburbs. Sites were still needed for new schools, especially secondary ones, as the baby-boomers began to move upwards to that level. Within the life of the diocese, he continued to head up the church extension programme, even though he and Bishop Luxton still disagreed over the right policy to be followed.

Although he had removed himself from all General Synod committees, he still kept an eye on National Church activities. An event on the national scene in 1964 gave him the opportunity to display his old mettle. The National Executive Council had prepared a brief for submission to the federal Royal Commission on Bilingualism and Biculturalism. Townshend obtained a copy of a draft. Appalled and shocked by what he read, he penned a lengthy critique of it. From the opening paragraph of his rebuttal he found almost nothing to praise.

> The Brief is definitely pro-French. It takes for granted...that the English and French languages are to co-exist on an equal basis in Canada for evermore. Its message appears to be that when everyone can understand both English and French, a "Canadian identity" and, therefore, perfect bliss can be achieved. It seems to me that the writers felt themselves bound to bend over backwards to laud and appease the French and to promote the French language. They appear to know even less than I do about the history of Canada.[84]

He went on to describe the brief as a "morass of self-praise, self-condemnation, would-be-high-sounding (but meaningless) phrases, misunderstandings and inaccuracies". In sum, "as an official Church document the Brief [sic] is disappointing. It lacks punch; it lacks conviction. It contains a few examples of ineffective preaching, which are sadly misplaced; and completely overlooks its big opportunity to speak as a church."[85]

Then he flayed virtually every paragraph in similar phraseology. When the authors of the brief stated that the function of all Canadian churches was to promote a society that recognized both founding cultures, Townshend's wrath knew no bounds.

> I take strong issue with this. The function of the Churches is to bring man to a knowledge and love of God, obedience to His will, and acceptance of salvation through Jesus Christ. This, as I see it, should be a full-time job! If the Churches would reach this goal of bringing men to Christ, there would be no cultural or lingual [sic] difficulties for them to fuss about.

He found almost nothing to praise, and in some places his language bordered on the vituperative, especially when he referred to the Francophones as "the Frenchies". Undoubtedly, many Church people agreed with his strictures but, on the whole, his scathing blast did not put him in the best light.

The fact of the matter was that Townshend, as with so many Anglophones of his generation, did not understand the immense changes taking place in Quebec. The Canada in which he grew up, with its emphasis on all things Anglo-Saxon, was passing away. Not only were the Francophones seeking to expand their role in Canadian life, particularly in Ottawa, but so were other minority groups. Canada was rapidly being transformed into a bilingual and multicultural society. It was hard for him to see the old landmarks cast aside. They had been his touchstones for many decades. It was difficult to adjust. For the rest of his life he would be uneasy about these policies. Besides, he constantly asked, who was behind it all? Was the hidden hand that of Rome?

However, he no longer exercised as much influence on the national scene as he once did. His activities were now mainly confined to the diocesan level. At Synod in 1965 he proposed another set of guidelines for church extension. "Perhaps the time has come when serious consideration should be given to a new policy whereby Church Extension moneys would be used for the purpose of enlarging, if necessary, the Clergy Staff of our existing Churches in the vicinity of the new subdivisions."[86] Here was the germ of a novel and potentially useful approach, but again it ran counter to Luxton's visionary expansion ideas.

As it was, Townshend was not to be involved with trying to develop the new scheme.[87] A short notice in that year's *Synod Journal* indicated that his health was troubling him again. "The Bishop expressed the best wishes of the House [sic] to the Right Reverend W.A. Townshend regarding his forthcoming surgery, and assured him of the full support of our prayers."[88]

His diabetes was worsening, and cataracts had begun to develop in his eyes, making it almost impossible to do any useful work. As he told the Rev. Howard Hamilton, a former student minister at the Church of the Redeemer who was now a rector in New York City, "I have to take insulin orally now, three times a day; and I have been having some nasty little pains which I don't like."[89] Surgery was absolutely necessary, and it had to be followed by a long period of recuperation. The operation was successful, but as he told Archbishop O'Neil of Fredericton, "I find the inactivity rather hard going. I cannot participate in any Service until September—no driving the car—no reading—no writing."[90] In spite of his recovery, it soon became apparent that his days in the active ministry were drawing to a close.

Shortly after the operation, one of his daughters, Eleanor, died. She had developed cancer several years earlier, but had recovered and appeared to be completely cured. Suddenly, in July, 1966 she contracted a severe virus which the doctors could not bring under control, and she passed away quickly. To add to the tragedy, her husband had suffered a coronary a few weeks before her death. The family was shocked by the suddenness of these events, but drew together in their grief—seeking solace in their Christian faith. As Townshend told several friends who wrote letters of condolence, "At such a time one's Christian faith does mean so much."[91]

HIS HEALTH PROBLEMS, Eleanor's death, and other matters culminated in a decision to retire.[92] Townshend gave notice that he was going to do so in April, 1967 at the end of his leave of absence. At its meeting in May, 1966, Synod paid tribute to his extensive work for the Church. A lengthy motion was passed, stating

> that the members of the 107th Synod of the Diocese of Huron here assembled desire to express their deep appreciation for the distinguished service which he has given to the Church in this Diocese, in the Ecclesiastical Province and in the Dominion. We wish to recognize the contribution that Bishop Townshend has made to our diocese in his 50 years of service, not only as Priest, as Diocesan Commissioner, as Secretary-Treasurer, but also as Suffragan Bishop. His kindly approach to all our people has been deeply appreciated by both the clergy and lay members of our Synod. He has contributed of his wisdom in financial matters to the benefit of the Diocese and the Church at large. He has also made a spiritual impact upon innumerable people in his long and fruitful ministry.[93]

Then, in a gracious gesture, Synod passed another motion permitting him to purchase the house in which he had lived during his episcopate for the price of the unpaid part of the mortgage.[94]

So it was over. Forty years of continuous labour for the Church he loved so much. Memories flooded in during those last few days before retirement became official, as did a host of letters, cards, and phone calls from well-wishers. They came from all corners of society—from ecclesiastical leaders in his own and other denominations, from parish priests, from laity, from businessmen, from colleagues in the educational world, and from politicians. The net was cast widely.

Retired and fully recovered from his surgery, what was he going to do with his spare time? First, there was the family. The numerous grandchildren would soon be joined by a growing flock of great-grandchildren. There were requests from other bishops to help with confirmation services. He was still a member of the school board. The cottage in Bayfield beckoned. Maybe he could do some reading. The house was commodious, and fortunately had a large back yard in which he could plant a garden. In fact, "Farmer Bill" could hardly wait to start digging in that rich soil. For much of the remainder of his life (and that was to be another 22 years) one of his greatest joys was to plant those seeds, especially the potatoes, every spring and then carefully tend them, watch them grow, and harvest them in the fall in time for the Church's annual service of Harvest Festival. He also managed to feed his own family and contribute to the tables of many of his vast throng of friends.

IN DECEMBER, 1966, Townshend again offered himself as a candidate in the school-board election. As he had been a consistent winner since 1934, he assumed that he would be successful again. But such was not the case. The London municipal elections witnessed a number of upsets that year. Both the public and separate boards garnered a number of new members. Among the defeated candidates was Townshend, who placed ninth in the tally, while his longtime colleague, C.C. Carrothers, came in second to last. Four younger people had replaced the old guard. As the *Free Press* expressed it, "After a day of upsets, education goes young."[95] Townshend was devastated by the rebuff. He had not expected it. How had it happened?

The *Free Press* described the election as "one of the most emotional—and exciting—races in the educational field in years."[96] Two or three reasons might account for his defeat. Townshend never spent very much money on campaign advertising, but this year some of the winners had adopted the modern technique of "selling oneself" that was becoming popular with politicians. Moreover, he had not totally recovered from his operation nor his bereavement over Eleanor. His old energy and enthusiasm flagged during this period; perhaps he was not ready for a stiff political battle. Lastly, change was in the air in the late sixties. Everyone talked about the need for change. One of the successful candidates, Bill Buchner, said, "There have been big changes. But I believe that now this is changing. I interpret the vote as an expression of the awakened interest of the parent."[97] Apparently many voters did not trust people like Townshend and Carrothers, members of an older generation, to implement the type of reforms the public now wanted. For the moment at least, the veterans were swept from the field.

CHAPTER SIX

The Years of Retirement

Retirement began differently than Townshend had originally anticipated. School board meetings, which would have occupied many hours, were now gone. What might fill this vacuum? He need not have worried. Requests to preach on special occasions and for various anniversaries quickly accumulated. In February, 1967 Bishop Snell of Toronto asked him to help with confirmation services in his diocese. Townshend quickly responded, "I will enjoy doing this, because there was nothing in my Episcopate I enjoyed more than the confirmations. It brings out all my old school-teacher instincts."[1] Originally they decided that he would conduct the services in two city churches, St. Hilda's and St. David's, and three in towns outside of Toronto. Townshend also told Snell that he would be delighted to preside at confirmations in the towns of Lindsay, Sutherland, Cannington and Beaverton, places he was familiar with from the days 40 years before when he had been a teacher in Manilla. He also mentioned a number of former Huron clergy who were now in the diocese of Toronto for whom he would like to conduct confirmations.[2]

Townshend requested that he and Kathleen, who was to accompany him, be given rooms at the Shelby House, where he usually stayed when he was in Toronto. However, Bishop Snell felt that the King Edward Hotel in the downtown area was more fitting for a visiting prelate. Kathleen agreed with this suggestion because, as Townshend told Snell's secretary, it was "much more convenient for shopping". Townshend jokingly added that he was "not quite sure that the convenience for shopping is just as good an idea as Mrs. Townshend thinks."[3] Townshend also indicated that, for the out-of-city services, they would stay with his old Huron County chum, the Rev. John

Thompson, who was a rector in Willowdale. After all, Townshend added humorously, "I was his baby-sitter on many occasions and no charge was made."[4]

During the next few weeks letters went back and forth between Townshend and the various rectors, arranging the details of the services.[5] Invariably Kathleen and he were invited to dinner at the rectories, and they gladly accepted. While in the town of Elmvale for a service, they hoped to visit a former school friend, Mrs. Fred Ritchie, to "have a chat about those dear old school days in Bayfield."[6] Trust Townshend to find a friend in yet another town!

So, during May and June they tended to these engagements, heartily enjoying the hospitality of the clergy and the congregations. Townshend was amazed at the size of the congregations which attended the mid-week confirmation services. As he told Bishop Snell, "We cannot get them to go to Church in the Diocese of Huron like that on a week night."[7] At the end of the tour he submitted a record to Bishop Snell, indicating that he had confirmed over 200 candidates. Instead of the original five services he had been scheduled to take, the number had swelled to eight. He requested reimbursement for his expenses and "any small honorarium that the Diocese of Toronto pay their visiting Bishops would be most gratefully received by a retired Bishop who is trying to live on 215 dollars a month."[8] Perhaps now he understood the reason why so many teachers' groups and clerics had expressed their appreciation to him for the many efforts he had made in securing pension benefits for them.

In between his trips to Toronto, he also performed a confirmation service for the clergy at St. John's Episcopal Church, Detroit, Michigan. One of the members of St. John's clerical staff, the Rev. C.H. Groh, a former priest of the Diocese of Huron, asked Townshend if he would conduct a confirmation at St. John's Church. Bishop Emrich of Michigan gave his permission.[9] Townshend was astonished to discover that the Episcopal service was "completely different from ours."[10] A few days after this event he was back in Toronto to take another confirmation. This one was held at St. Elizabeth's and was a combined service with the parish of St. Augustine.[11]

He was involved with this type of ecclesiastical duty for the remainder of his active life. The events of the winter and spring of 1967 set a pattern which he continued, with great enjoyment, for almost another 20 years.[12]

AFTER ANOTHER RESTFUL summer at the cottage in Bayfield, the Townshends returned to their city home where the garden needed tending and harvesting. In the autumn of 1967 the Board of Education appointed him to the newly created Educational Advisory Council.[13] One of the new trustees, Dr. Stanley French, thought it might be useful to bring together a number of people interested in education to "study, and if advisable, make recommendations and/or reports to the Board of Education on any matters concerning the education of students."[14] The committee was, in many ways, a reflection of the spirit of the late sixties, an exercise in participatory democracy. Very little was contributed by this group to the board's activities, however. Townshend remained a member until he was re-elected as a trustee in 1969.

By the time he returned to the board in that year, the contours of the educational landscape had begun to be reshaped. The curriculum, pedagogical methods, and the organization of Ontario's public schools were all being transformed by innovative concepts and techniques. The justification and rationale for these changes was contained in a new report entitled *Living and Learning* (popularly referred to as the Hall-Dennis Report), which quickly became a manual for educational reformers throughout the province. In 1965 the Department of Education appointed a committee to review and revise the curriculum for Grades 1 to 6. Composed of 21 members, virtually all of whom were drawn from the elementary panel, the group was presided over by Mr. Justice Emmett Hall, who was later joined by Mr. Lloyd Dennis, an elementary-school principal from Toronto. Dennis—who had long been an advocate of a more open, flexible style of teaching and learning—exercised a strong influence over the committee and its work.

Although its original terms of reference had restricted the committee's scope to the lower grades, it soon realized that its recommendations could not be so limited. Permission was granted for the committee to extend its sphere of activity to include the high school.

Consequently, the report, when it was published in 1968, profoundly affected virtually every aspect of Ontario's public schools.

As one commentator has written, "The Hall-Dennis report [sic] was hailed by many, perhaps even by most, as a significant step forward in the history of Ontario education. It called upon the principles set out in the Universal Declaration of Human Rights, reiterated the aims of education put forward in the *Report* of the Royal Commission on Education in Ontario, 1950, and came out strongly in favour of a child centred philosophy of education."[15] It was this latter trait which captured the public's imagination. In the words of the report itself:

> One of the fundamental issues facing Ontario schools is the shift of focus from structured content to the child, or young person, as an individual learner. The change, already under way, has many ramifications. The graded system, as a succession of achievement levels, will be abandoned in favour of continuous progress by the pupil. The concept of passing or failing and of being promoted or made to repeat a year will disappear. The schools that are envisaged will give every pupil an opportunity to participate in selecting and planning his studies. Emphasis upon the needs and interests of the individual child is the very essence of this report.[16]

The report reflected the spirit of North American society in the late 1960s—with all the flamboyance of the counter-culture, the hippies and flower children with their love-ins, their relaxed style of dress, and their slogan of "make love not war". Staid Ontario has never seen a report like it. It was a lavish publication with dozens of photographs of smiling, happy children learning and playing in bright, cheery class-rooms or out on field trips pursuing some exotic goal. The prose was equally upbeat, revelling in romanticism and glowing word pictures of children and their assumed desire to absorb all of the learning their social and physical environments had to offer. The report clearly reflected the feelings of that period, which, no doubt, is one of the major reasons it immediately became popular. Few detractors raised their voices in dissent, and those who did were summarily shouted down. It was a magnificent exercise in rhetoric and sloganeering!

Even though the government never officially adopted the *Hall-Dennis Report*, its spirit and myriad recommendations quickly began to penetrate the school system. At the elementary level much of the child-centred philosophy had been the norm for some time. It was upon the secondary school that the report ultimately had its most significant impact. For in the spring of 1969 a new version of the high-school programme was issued by the Department. This scheme was the work of another internal department committee.[17]

The essential purpose of this new system was to permit each student to build a profile of credits towards a graduation certificate. Twenty-seven credits were needed to graduate from Grade 12, 33 from Grade 13. The onus for choosing these credits rested on the student and parents. School officials were simply to assist in making these decisions. Gone were the various tracks and the multitude of programmes which had been introduced earlier in the decade. Now all courses were of equal value. There was a blurring of the distinction between academic and technical 'programmes' as students were allowed to enroll in any of them. In the new world of equality this seemed only just.

What was Townshend's reaction to the report and the new high-school programme? Since he had not yet been re-elected as a member of the board, he did not have a public platform from which to voice his views. It was not until he had returned as a trustee and had become embroiled a few years later in a messy dispute over corporal punishment that he lashed out publicly at the *Hall-Dennis Report*. Yet it is not difficult to surmise what his attitude would have been right from the outset. He totally rejected its materialistic, hedonistic philosophical basis. Such an approach was hardly in keeping with his style of Christianity, which many people of the day probably labelled as being old-fashioned and out of step with contemporary values. But to Townshend the apparent absence of any reference to Christian virtues (which the *Hope Report* had contained) was deplorable. Moreover, the impetus this new report seemed to give towards the creation of a permissive society was dangerous, and in the long run society itself would suffer serious damage. Basically, the style and value-positions of the sixties were utterly foreign to the ageing bishop. These were not the principles and values he had learned from his mother so long ago in Bayfield or from Principal Waller at Huron College. Society was setting out on a different course, and the outcomes were, in his mind, not going to be very beneficial. As so often happens in history, a young leader with liberal or advanced ideas, as Townshend had been, is overtaken and ignored by those who succeed him, to be left virtually alone with his successes and his thoughts.

The London Board, for example, had submitted a brief to the Hall-Dennis committee in 1966, as did numerous other boards, groups and individuals. It bore no resemblance to the one Townshend had overseen 20 years earlier for the Hope Commission. The manner of its development and its recommendations were both distinctly different from its predecessor. Its style and tone resembled the *Hall-Dennis Report* itself, with a call for child-centred classrooms, a wider curriculum, the abolition of corporal punishment, and other trendy nostrums. It lacked the specificity that the Townshend document had possessed, and certainly did not receive the same kind of reception from the committee as the earlier one had. Townshend, it seems, had little involvement with its composition.[18]

THE PUBLIC HAD BARELY been given time to digest the radical Hall-Dennis proposals when the government introduced two more sweeping innovations. The thrust of the first was to eliminate the incredibly large number of school boards that abounded in Ontario. For many years officials in the Department of Education had regarded the plethora of small boards and their attendant schools not only as inefficient and wasteful but as a major barrier in implementing a policy of equality of educational opportunity across the province. Over the years the number of one-room schools had been replaced with larger consolidated ones. This, in turn, meant that their boards disappeared from the administrative structure. Although this policy created enormous resentment in many rural areas, the government continued to push ahead with it, and in 1969 introduced the final phase. New boards based on the county as the governing unit became the norm. Six cities, including London, retained their individual boards, but the number of trustees was increased. London's complement rose from six to twelve.

This action certainly diluted the amount of power and influence any one trustee wielded.

The other significant alteration for Ontario public education emerged from the recommendations made by the Committee on Religious Education in the Public Schools of the Province of Ontario. Headed by the former lieutenant-governor, J. Keiller MacKay, this group had tackled the emotional issue of religious instruction in the schools. Faced by an increasing number of non-Christian faiths and an apparently more secularized society, many parents and pressure groups had begun to complain about the courses which imparted instruction in the tenets of Christianity. After reviewing the issue, the MacKay Committee advocated discontinuing the present syllabus, which had been introduced in 1944. Yet, the committee argued that schools should continue to help children develop an ethical code. Teaching moral values was, in its estimation, preferable to trying to inculcate religious doctrine, and hopefully would not generate as much public criticism. A course in comparative religion, the report suggested, might be offered on the senior high-school level. For all of its calm tone and mild assertions, the report was something of a bombshell. Many of its critics saw it as an overt attempt to divorce education from religion, a tie which went back to the early days of the province, and had been a part of the public school system since its inception in the middle decades of the previous century.

How did Townshend react to these developments? Unfortunately, there are few recorded specific comments, but it is clear, as will shortly be noted, that he thoroughly disapproved of the philosophy of the *Hall-Dennis Report* and the *MacKay Report*. In his estimation, the former was much too progressive, while the latter was a disaster. Both were a reflection of the increasing materialism and selfishness which he saw pervading current society. He distrusted these attitudes, fearing they would weaken and perhaps destroy the basis of contemporary life.

The London board moved quickly to implement some of the new proposals. Hardly had the *MacKay Report* been published when the trustees decided to discontinue the current course in religious education. After securing permission from the Ministry of Education (as the Department was now called), the board announced that the subject would be dropped from the public schools in September, 1969. In its place the *MacKay Report*'s approach for the teaching of moral values was adopted.[19] The die was cast! No longer would children in London's elementary schools take courses in religious education which had a distinctly Christian emphasis.

To Townshend this was nonsense! In fact, it brought him back into the public arena. He decided to run again for the board in the forthcoming municipal elections. This time he put more money and effort into campaigning and advertising his views, especially on religious education. Apparently many voters agreed with him, as he was returned to his old seat with a substantial majority.[20] But it was all very different this time around. The board was not only larger, as previously noted, but the other members were younger and had, by and large, been influenced by the new concepts in education. In a word, many of them, like the voters they represented, had been influenced by that elusive creature, "the spirit of the times". They saw things differently than the Bishop did. Moreover, none of his old allies was there with him.

These factors made it difficult for Townshend to promote his ideas as successfully as he had in previous days. With a doubling of the number of trustees, power was diffused, and his former base of authority was missing. While he could still exert some influence behind the scenes, he no longer dominated the board's proceedings. His "golden day" had passed.

Nonetheless, he served for another ten years. He was often a member of the Vocational Advisory Committee and the Business and Property Committee—two of his perennial interests—but even here things were different from the old days, especially with the former group. And while the property committee continued to acquire new sites in the early seventies, he was no longer its czar. In fact, when this committee became embroiled in the very emotional and difficult task of closing some inner-city schools, he had hardly anything to say. Similarly, in vocational education new developments had passed him by, and his voice was largely muted in discussions. He became a "passive observer" of the scene.[21]

While the board struggled with financial difficulties, provincially imposed spending ceilings, declining enrollments, the new credit system

Townshend shortly after his ordination as bishop.

TOP: *The family in 1955. BACK ROW: Jim, Betty, Mary, Peggy, Bill, Bob. CENTRE ROW: John, Mrs. Townshend, the Bishop, Eleanor. FRONT ROW: Barbara and Nancy.*

BOTTOM: *The University of Western Ontario Convocation, 1960: Townshend, Rev. Alexander Nimmo, Arthur Ford, and Greg Clark.*

LEFT: *Townshend ordaining son Bob, June 4, 1960 at the Church of the Redeemer.*

RIGHT: *Speaking for the retention of corporal punishment at the meeting of the London Board of Education, February 17, 1972.*

Forty-four years completed! Townshend's announcement of his retirement as a school-board trustee, October 7, 1980.

in the secondary schools, growing teacher militancy, and a myriad of other problems, Townshend preferred to concentrate on two other issues which he felt were important—religious education and discipline. Many people, both in London and other cities, deplored the demise of religious education. To them, its removal had created a vacuum in the curriculum. Interestingly, even though London had withdrawn this subject from its schools, a few trustees felt that some form of religious education should be retained. A committee, with Townshend as a member, was struck to investigate the matter. After an intensive review it recommended that "the emphasis should be placed on Morals and Ethics, rather than religion."[22] Yet, at the same time in what sounded like a contradictory move, the report went on to state, "The proposed study of moral values, as recommended by this committee, should not be viewed as an alternative to the study of religion; indeed, it is hoped that more positive programmes in religion, which will greatly enhance the study of values, will soon be possible."[23] It is not clear what the committee had in mind. At any rate, this was as far as it was prepared to go in addressing the concern. The Bishop accepted the basic thrust of the report; at least it gave students some form of character education. But he pined for a return to his own conception of religious instruction.

HARDLY HAD THE DEBATE over this issue died down when an equally emotional topic began to occupy the board's time and energy. The *Hall-Dennis Report* had condemned the use of the strap and called for its elimination. Trustees and others who had accepted the report's philosophy were anxious to implement this recommendation in London. Their campaign was supported by many child psychologists, individual teachers (especially on the elementary level), and some parents.

It was a topic guaranteed to generate a lot of heat, as the London trustees were about to discover. A motion was presented to abolish the use of the strap in London schools at a board meeting on February 12, 1972. Every trustee was given the opportunity to state his/her opinion. Townshend vigorously lashed out against this proposal. The next day's edition of the *Free Press* carried a photograph of him standing at the podium with his arm upraised and his forefinger pointing to heaven like an Old Testament prophet predicting doom and destruction.[24] Proper discipline, he asserted, was one of the major lessons children must acquire early in life, and the school had an important role to play in this endeavour. Good discipline had been declining in the schools in recent years, he claimed. "I believe it's been going downhill every since the Hall-Dennis Report came out. In my opinion...the Hall-Dennis Report has rendered the greatest disservice to education in this province in the last 100 years. Without discipline in the classroom, you have no learning situation at all."[25] To support the abolishment of corporal punishment, he thundered, was to indicate a lack of confidence in the administration and the teachers.

This was an ironic stance for a father who claimed that he never spanked any of his ten children. Yet he felt very strongly about this issue. Teachers, he argued, needed the threat of the strap if they were to maintain a proper learning environment. Look at the antics of current high-school students. And the activities of university students with their protests and marches was even worse. Law and order, the essentials of a good society to a conservative, appeared to be crumbling as political leaders throughout the Western world capitulated before the noisy demands of youth. The educational system was betraying its students in not instilling discipline. At the heart of the breakdown of authority in Ontario's schools was that ridiculous *Hall-Dennis Report*. There was the real culprit! Townshend's analysis of the situation, while it was simplistic in many respects, was widely held among the public, and the Bishop received much support for his stand.

However, in spite of his strictures and those of other trustees, and the support of the local teachers' federations, corporal punishment was abolished in London schools.[26] But, as it turned out, this was not the end of the matter. The topic kept resurfacing; like a bad penny it would not go away. Hardly a year passed during the remainder of the decade when corporal punishment was not discussed at a board meeting. Townshend continued to be one of the voices calling for its reinstitution. Finally, in 1975, a motion, which Townshend happily seconded, was placed before the trustees calling for the reintroduction of the strap. After considerable debate it was suggested that a series of guidelines be composed to govern its use.[27] Once these had been approved by the board, the use of the strap was permitted, albeit on a limited basis.[28] For the remainder of his time of service with the board, corporal punishment was permissible.

Townshend's attitude should not be seen in a totally negative light. After all, as has been noted, while he may not have spanked his own children, he certainly had received many beatings from his father when he was a youngster. He was certain in his own mind that such punishment had not harmed him. Rather, he had learned one of the most important lessons that life had to offer—that consequences follow improper actions. Children needed to absorb this dictum, and corporal punishment was one way of their doing so. Moreover, society required law-abiding citizens, people who not only respected law and order but who were willing to enforce it in their own homes.

HIS FULMINATIONS ABOUT religious education and discipline, however, did not cast a shadow over the many successful campaigns he had waged in his long career to improve other areas of education. Certain groups still remembered his many positive contributions. To honour Townshend on his 80th birthday and to express their appreciation for his many efforts on behalf of teachers, the local branch of the O.S.S.T.F. established an award in his name, to be given to the secondary-school teacher, vice-principal, or principal who best exemplified the Bishop's philosophy of education.[29] A year later the Faculty of Education at the University of Western Ontario created the Townshend Medal to be awarded to the leading graduate in the Master of Education programme at both the spring and fall convocations.[30] Until almost his last year, the Bishop was on hand to present this award to the winners, and give them warm words of encouragement.

Aside from the two heated battles, mentioned earlier, Townshend's last years on the board were relatively inactive. By the end of the decade he had become tired of such service. He was now over 80 years old. Perhaps it was time to leave the struggle to others. Why not step aside and enjoy the few years that remained to him and Kathleen? At the conclusion of the board's meeting on October 7, 1980, he surprised his fellow trustees by announcing that he would not be running in the forthcoming election. In a short speech which recounted many of the highlights of his time on the board, he told them,

> It is a real wrench to leave the Board of Education. I will always hold as very precious the memory of the fellowship of many fellow trustees for whom I had and have great respect and admiration for their able, devoted, and inspirational leadership in the field of education. The educational well-being of girls and boys must be the first concern of every good trustee.[31]

However, he could not resist making one final plea for the reinstatement of religious education.

> One regret I have in leaving the Board is not seeing religious education or Bible teaching established again in our system. It was introduced into our system in 1937 on my motion, and for 32 years religious education flourished in our midst. There was a very close working co-operation on the part of home, school and church. I felt it was a great loss to our City of London when it was thrown out by the Board in 1969. May the new Board seriously consider bringing it back for blessed is the nation whose God is the Lord.[32]

His astonished colleagues quickly recovered, and passed a resolution unanimously expressing "their sincere appreciation to Rt. Rev. W.A. Townshend for his lifetime of service to the education of children in London". To this motion they appended the sentence, "No man stands taller than when he stoops to help a child."[33] Individual trustees paid tribute to his work, while the Director of Education, Dr. Madeleine Hardy, summed up the feelings of many when she said, "You have left the unique and strong stamp of your personality on this board."[34]

The board graciously followed this tribute with a banquet honouring Townshend for his long service to the cause of education. It was a happy occasion with a number of speakers recalling episodes from his long career. Premier Davis sent a special certificate of long service, while the Hon. Gordon Walker, M.P.P. for London South, recounted the story of Townshend's foray into provincial politics in 1937 and his close affiliation with various Tory leaders over the years. A special brochure outlining his many contributions to education on the local and provincial scenes was prepared by Tom Moore, Executive Secretary of the Board, and was given to those in attendance. At the end of the evening, Townshend thanked everyone for attending. "You have done me a great honour with your presence here tonight."[35]

ANOTHER MILESTONE had been passed. All his ties with public life were now cut. It was time to sit back and reflect on his long and busy career, and to enjoy leisure time with Kathleen and the ever-expanding family. But idleness was not his way. He kept up a busy round of engagements, especially if Clinton or Bayfield had something special going on and asked him to participate. There was still that large garden to tend, and friends continued to drop in to "chin-wag" about the old days. He still attended meetings of the diocesan Synod, where he kept abreast of the activities of the clergy he had ordained. He keenly watched the progress of the younger ones, including his son Bob, who was rapidly rising in the Church. The decision of one of his grandsons, Peter, to enter the priesthood made him very happy.

Another major event in his life occurred in December, 1981, when Kathleen and he celebrated their diamond wedding anniversary. Their marriage and life together was a remarkable achievement and an equally remarkable union. Here they were—that high-spirited little boy and that cute little girl—60 years later, surrounded by nine of their ten children and a host of relatives and friends, celebrating that wedding held so long ago on a cold day in December, 1921. The anniversary festivities were held on December 18, another cold and snowy day. It began with a Holy Communion service in the chapel of Huron College, followed by a family dinner and then a gala reception in the Great Hall, attended by a large number of well-wishers. It was an immensely enjoyable event, especially with so many grandchildren and great grandchildren present. As it turned out, it was the last major episode of their long lives, for Kathleen received her home-call two years later.

Now he was truly alone. He had his home, his garden, and his memories, but it was lonely without Kathleen. Still, there were bright moments. Undoubtedly, the happiest one was the election of Bob to be a Suffragan Bishop in the Diocese of Huron, the post he once held. On September 12, 1984, the old bishop once more climbed into the pulpit of St. Paul's Cathedral where he had so often spoke. This time he was preaching at his son's consecration as a bishop, a unique event in Canadian Anglican history. In a strong voice, he counselled his son that a bishop "must be a priest, a prophet, a shepherd and a friend. I trust Robert has all four qualities."[36] At the end of his sermon, a touching scene occurred. As the ageing bishop descended from the pulpit, Bob stepped over and embraced his father. It was another remarkable day, marred only by Kathleen's absence.

Just over a year later, in November, 1985, he celebrated the 30th anniversary of his own consecration. In an interview with the *London Free Press*, he told a reporter that he had preached to a congregation of 1,650 people at Holmesville (near Clinton) in July and had delivered another sermon to a packed church in Waterford earlier in November. He indicated he had no intention of slowing down. His mother, he said, had taught him and his brothers that, "We Townshends never give up in life. We just keep right on keeping on."[37] And for the remainder of his life that was his attitude.

Two years later his health began to decline, and he became bedridden. On Sunday, January 17, 1988, he breathed his last, and received his home-call. A life of dedicated service had come to a close. The funeral service was held at St. Paul's Cathedral on January 20, 1988. The cathedral was filled with the friends and colleagues of past years. The service was conducted by the Rt. Rev. Derwyn Jones, Bishop of Huron, assisted by the Most Rev. Michael Peers, Primate of Canada, the Most Rev. John Bothwell, Archbishop of Niagara, and Suffragan Bishop Percy O'Driscoll of Huron. The lessons were read by his son-in-law, the Rev. Canon Robert Foster, and his grandson, the Rev. Peter Townshend. Archdeacon John Morden, his old colleague at Huron College, gave the eulogy. Then he was interred in the grave next to Kathleen in Mt. Pleasant Cemetery.

YEARS EARLIER, IN WRITING to a friend sick in a hospital, Townshend had said, "Yours has been, indeed, a very abundant life. The important thing in life is how 'much' we live, not how 'long'."[38] This remark could easily be an epithet for Townshend's own life. Though he had lived longer than most people do, his life had indeed been abundant. His contributions to his Church and to education were truly remarkable. In many areas, especially in education, he was ahead of his time, and it took years for others to flesh out his proposals. As Archdeacon Morden said in his homily, "But despite these many achievements it was as a good pastor that Bishop William Alfred Townshend will remain in our hearts."[39]

Townshend's career in education and the Church as a teacher, pastor, trustee and ecclesiastical administrator spanned almost six decades. It had been exhilarating, arduous, frustrating, joyful; it had canvassed the whole range of human emotions. In retrospect, what had he accomplished? Educational leaders and teachers had heaped praise on his vision of education, even though by the end of his tenure some of its features were regarded as outmoded. Teachers' organizations and support-staff groups lauded his constant efforts to obtain better working conditions for them—improved salaries, benefit packages, pensions, a measure of pay equity for women, sabbaticals, and a host of others. The purpose of the educational enterprise for Townshend was to educate the whole child, to prepare children and adolescents for more abundant living. All aspects of the person—intellectual, spiritual, physical and social—were of equal importance, and had to be cultivated. Nor was this simply an idealistic attitude to be trotted out for public speeches. There was in it a genuine concern for youth's economic future. Townshend was noted for his advocacy of vocational education long before it became fashionable in the 1960s. Early in his career as a trustee, he began to campaign for a wholesale revision of the high-school programme to make a secondary education which was responsive, relevant and practical for that vast majority of students who would not attend the collegiate institute whose curriculum was too weighted in favour of the "academic" minority. Education, he held, was needed by all sectors of the population; it should not be confined to a select few. While he certainly respected the scholarship embodied in the Ontario high-school tradition, his view of schooling was infused with a utilitarian ethos. The heart of his "radical" campaign in the 1940s and his work with the Hope Commission reflected this attitude. No child or adolescent, including the handicapped, should be neglected. He was an early supporter of providing education for this latter group, and maintained this interest until the end of his service as a trustee. Calling Townshend a prophet might be something of an exaggeration, and certainly he himself would have demurred, but at the very least he was a forward-looking leader in educational affairs.

The Church, of course, was his first love. It was to this form of service that he had originally been called. Yet all during his clerical career, many of the issues he handled in the Church were similar to those he encountered in the educational field. Providing a decent mode of life for the clergy and their families was always uppermost in his mind. Proper rectories, stipends, and pensions were issues to which he paid careful attention. The entire financial structure of the Church was his bailiwick, and, while many people felt he pursued it too zealously, there is no question that he improved the financial situation of the Diocese of Huron and, in doing so, made Church people more aware of the Church's needs. Almost single-handedly he injected a more enthusiastic spirit into the total life of the diocese and its administration after the grey years of the 1930s. His administrative abilities were harnessed by the National Church, which placed him on numerous committees, especially those dealing with finances. He rarely refused a request to serve on another committee. Undoubtedly his single most important contribution to the National Church was his role in designing a new pension scheme for the clergy. Townshend was not cast in the mold of a mystic or a theologian. He was foremost a pastor and an administrator, and it was these gifts (or charisms to use a New Testament word) which he used for the betterment of church and school. But, above all, it was people with whom he was primarily concerned, not their institutions. His was a people-oriented career.

Notes

Abbreviations and Shortened References

CRA	Church of the Redeemer Archives
DHA	Diocese of Huron Archives
HCA	Huron College Archives
LBE	London Board of Education
LFP	*London Free Press*
OA	Ontario Archives
ST	Susan Townshend (taped interviews)
UWO	The University of Western Ontario
WAT	William A. Townshend (papers)
WT	William Townshend (taped interviews)

INTRODUCTION

1. Quoted in Leon Edel, *Writing Lives: Prinicipia Biographia* (New York, 1984), title page.
2. Quoted in Robert Skidelsky, "Only Connect: Biography and Truth", in Eric Homberger and John Charmley, *The Troubled Face of Biography* (New York, 1988), p. 1.
3. Eric Homberger and John Charmley, op. cit., p. 1. Note the intriguing title of this book.
4. For a discussion of this attitude see David Novarr, *The Lines of Life: Theories of Biography, 1880-1970* (West Lafayette, Indiana, 1986), pp. xi-xiv.
5. Francis West, *Biography as History* (Sydney, 1973), p. 5.
6. Ibid., pp. 5-6.
7. Leon Edel, op. cit., p. 19.
8. Eric Homberger and John Charmley, op. cit., p. ix.
9. Quoted in Leon Edel, op. cit., pp. 19-20.
10. It is doubtful if Strachey reached this level himself. There are numerous errors of fact in his book and his interpretation of the characters has never been widely accepted.

11. Leon Edel, op. cit., p. 29.
12. For incisive critiques of the use of psychology in history see Jacques Barzun, *Clio and the Doctors: Psycho-History, Quanto-History and History* (Chicago, 1974) and David E. Stannard, *Shrinking History: On Freud and the Failure of Psychology* (New York, 1980).
13. Leon Edel, op. cit., p. 23.
14. Robert Craig Brown, "Biography in Canadian History", in Terry Crowley, *Clio's Craft, A Primer of Historical Methods* (Toronto, 1988), p. 160.

CHAPTER ONE

1. DHA, WAT papers, L file, W.A. Townshend to Ralph Lampman, R.R.#3, Florence, Ont., June 3, 1965.
2. Most of the material used in this chapter was drawn from interviews of Bishop W.A. Townshend conducted by William and Susan Townshend. The material on his ancestry is drawn from a letter from A.L. Crich, Sarnia, Ont. to the author, London, Ont., September 22, 1986.
3. Of the four sons, Ern remained on the farm; John became a teacher and later principal of a collegiate institute, and was killed during the Second World War; Alvin was trained as a civil engineer and became President and General Manager of Donland Inspection Company of Canada in Montreal; William, of course, became a teacher, priest and bishop.
4. ST interviews, pp. 2-3.
5. Ibid., p. 27.
6. Ibid., p. 12.
7. Ibid., p. 8.
8. Ibid., p. 19.
9. DHA, WAT papers, B file, W.A. Townshend to Bruce Briggs, Boys Farm, Ailsa Craig, Ont., May 21, 1966.
10. ST, p. 58.
11. Ibid., pp. 52-53.
12. Ibid., pp. 24-25.
13. J.J. Talman, *Huron College* (London, Ont., 1963).
14. F.H. Armstrong, *The Forest City* (Windsor, Ont., 1986), see chapts. 4 and 5.
15. UWO, Weldon Library, Regional History Room, collection of university calendars.
16. ST, pp. 123-130.
17. WT, interview #1, pp. 1-2.
18. Ibid., #2B, pp. 5-6.
19. ST, p. 142.

CHAPTER TWO

1. Philip Carrington, *The Anglican Church in Canada* (Toronto, 1963), p. 255.
2. Ibid., pp. 254-256.
3. Ibid., pp. 257-258.
4. John Webster Grant, *The Church in the Canadian Era*, 1st ed. (Toronto, 1972), p. 132.
5. DHA, Preacher's Book, Parish of St. John's, Bervie, Ont., August 1, 1926.
6. May Boyle, Kingarf, Ont., "The Reverend William A. Townshend", an essay composed for the author, June, 1986.
7. DHA, *Synod Journal*, 1928.
8. May Boyle, op. cit., n. p.
9. Ibid., n. p.
10. DHA, WAT papers, H file, Townshend to Rev. G.S. Honour, Marathon, Ont., April 7, 1960.
11. DHA, *Synod Journal*, 1929, pp. lxxvi-lxxvii.
12. WT, #4, pp. 15-16.
13. DHA, *Synod Journal*, 1930, p. 30.
14. CRA, Vestry Minute Book, 1926-1947, January 26, 1930.
15. Ibid.
16. ST, p. 114.
17. CRA has a collection of these invitations.
18. WT, #4, pp. 21-22.
19. *LFP*, December 5, 1933.
20. R.M. Stamp, *The Schools of Ontario* (Toronto, 1982), p. 143.
21. LBE *Minutes*, 1934, p. 3.
22. Ibid., p. 70.
23. Ibid., p. 122.
24. Ibid., p. 130.
25. Since he was re-elected approximately 20 times, each new term will not be noted.
26. LBE *Minutes*, 1935, pp. 246, 297.
27. R.M. Stamp, op.cit., pp. 150-154; Franklin Walker, *Catholic Education and Politics in Ontario*, Vol. II (Toronto, 1986), chapt. 14. Neil Mc-Henty, *Mitch Hepburn* (Toronto, 1967), pp. 76-84.
28. LBE *Minutes*, 1935, pp. 59-60 and *LFP*, February 14, 1935.
29. Townshend had also attempted to rally the support of the Diocesan Synod on this matter. See *Synod Journal*, 1936, p. 42.
30. Ibid., 1934, p. 35.
31. CRA, Minute Book of the Deanery of East Middlesex, various meetings, n. p.
32. CRA, Vestry Minute Book, January 25, 1937, n. p.
33. *LFP*, June 19 and 25, 1937.

34. The parishes of St. Mary's Walkerville in Windsor and St. John the Evangelist in Kitchener had both considered him as a possible rector. Seager had suggested him for the national office: DHA, Archbishop Seager papers, Seager to Ven. Archdeacon J.M. Snowden, M.A., D.D., Ottawa, October 19, 1937.
35. LBE *Minutes*, January 14, 1937, p. 6. The complete speech is carried on pp. 4-8.
36. Ibid.
37. Ibid., p. 330.
38. Ibid., p. 158.
39. Ibid., p. 304.
40. Ibid.
41. Ibid., p. 240.
42. CRA, Minutes of the Select Vestry, November 6, 1938.
43. *LFP*, September 11, 1937.
44. Ibid.
45. Ibid., October 5, 1937.
46. Ibid.
47. Ibid., October 7, 1937.
48. DHA, *Synod Journal*, 1938, pp. 27-28.
49. CRA, Minutes of the Select Vestry, November 6, 1938.
50. CRA, Annual Vestry Minutes, January 23, 1939.
51. HCA, Seager papers, Synod 1940 file, Seager to Townshend, November 2, 1938.

CHAPTER THREE

1. DHA, *Synod Journal*, 1939.
2. DHA, Minutes of the Executive Committee, December 15, 1938, pp. 645-647.
3. DHA, WAT papers, Diocesan Commission file, 1939, several entries.
4. DHA, *Synod Journal*, 1941, p. 91.
5. DHA, WAT papers, Diocesan Commissioner file, 1939, Bishop C. Seager to the Church Wardens of Florence, Aughrim and Bothwell, November 14, 1939.
6. LBE *Minutes*, 1939, p. 85. The entire report is reprinted on pp. 84-88.
7. Ibid., pp. 96, 97, 98, 103-104.
8. R.M. Stamp, op. cit., pp. 171-172.
9. LBE *Minutes*, 1940, p. 84.
10. Ibid., pp. 82, 84, 86, 104.
11. DHA, *Synod Journal*, 1940, Report of the Diocesan Commissioner, pp. 90-91.
12. DHA, *Synod Journal*, 1940, p. 94.
13. DHA, WAT papers, Diocesan Commission file, 1940, various entries.

14. DHA, *Synod Journal*, 1940, p. 91.
15. ST.
16. DHA, WAT papers, Diocesan Commission file, 1941, Bishop Seager to Rev. R.A.E. Ruch, Fort McMurray, Alta., January 17, 1941.
17. DHA, *Synod Journal*, 1941, Report of the Diocesan Commissioner, p. 91.
18. HCA, Minutes of the Huron College Council, December 16, 1941, p. 172.
19. Ibid., June 17, 1942, p. 181.
20. Ibid., February 2, 1943, p. 189.
21. Ibid., June 28, 1943, p. 195 and September 29, 1943, p. 198.
22. Ibid., December 16, 1943, p. 203. Curiously, at this same meeting, Townshend donated a prize of $5.00 to the student who submitted the best essay on the diocesan budget.
23. DHA, *Synod Journal*, 1941, Budget Committee Report, p. 84.
24. Ibid., p. 38.
25. Ibid., pp. 102-103.
26. DHA, WAT papers, Diocesan Commissioner file, 1941, Rev. Handley Perkins, St. Thomas, Ont. to Bishop Seager, March 28, 1941.
27. UWO, Senate Minutes, March 3, 1943.
28. Ibid., p. 22. Note the month was April not March.
29. *LFP*, January 10, 1941.
30. LBE *Minutes*, 1941, p. 14.
31. Ibid., pp. 116-118. The preamble to this report indicates that high-school teachers had been involved in its composition and that one university in the area, unnamed, had agreed to accept this certificate. Brescia Hall, since re-named Brescia College, was a Roman Catholic female college affiliated with the university. It offered a Home Economics degree.
32. Ibid., p. 130.
33. Ibid., p. 151.
34. Ibid., 1942, pp. 4-5.
35. There is something of a contradiction here. If Townshend and the trustees were trying to create a new certificate course for students who did not intend to go on to university, why was there a need to seek university approval of it unless this was a ploy to secure backing for a general revision of the entire high-school programme throughout the province?
36. Ibid., p. 5.
37. Ibid., 1942, pp. 4-5.
38. Ibid., p. 150.
39. There is no correspondence between Drew and Townshend on this matter in either the Townshend or Drew papers.
40. Edward Pulker, *We Stand On Their Shoulders* (Toronto, 1986), pp. 142-148.
41. LBE *Minutes*, 1944, p. 2.

42. Philip Carrington, op. cit., pp. 280- 281.
43. DHA, Minutes of the Executive Council, 1944, pp. 301-302.
44. Ibid.
45. DHA, *Synod Journal*, 1945, p. 95.
46. Ibid., p. 96.
47. Ibid., pp. 40-41.
48. DHA, Minutes of the Executive Committee, April 4, 1945, p. 349.
49. Ibid., April 9, 1945, pp. 387-388, 400.
50. DHA, *Synod Journal*, 1946, Report of the Finance Committee, p. 71.
51. Townshend was deeply involved in the acquisition of both properties.
52. DHA, Seager papers, Archdeacon file, several entries.
53. Ibid., Townshend to Archbishop Seager, London, July 2, 1945.
54. LBE *Minutes*, 1945, p. 2.
55. The work of the Royal Commission is discussed in the next chapter.

CHAPTER FOUR

1. J.W. Grant, op. cit., p. 160.
2. Ibid., p. 163.
3. C.F. Coulson, "An Historical Survey of Royal Commissions and Other Major Government Investigations in Education" (Ed.D. diss., University of Toronto 1966), pp. 380-381.
4. There is no documentary evidence in Townshend's papers or in any of the files consulted at the Ontario Archives to support this supposition, but it is not outside the realm of possibility. A local London source related to the author that had the Conservatives won the provincial election in 1937 and had Townshend also been successful, then he would have been virtually guaranteed the appointment as Minister of Education.
5. *Report of the Royal Commission on Education* (Toronto, 1950), p. vi.
6. R.M. Stamp, op. cit., p. 160.
7. LBE *Minutes*, January 3, 1946, pp. 2ff.
8. Ibid., December 12, 1946, p. 160.
9. Ibid., March 25, 1946, p. 45.
10. OA, RG 18 Commissions and Committees, Royal Commission on Education in Ontario (December 15, 1950), Proceedings, vol. 1. B-115, Box 1, p. 2380. (The entire brief is contained in pp. 2378-2418.)
11. This idea was probably borrowed from Great Britain where a similar type of school was being opened, although the London brief does not acknowledge this source of inspiration.
12. Ibid., p. 2410.
13. DHA, Seager papers, A Brief Submitted to the Ontario Royal Commission on Education by the Church of England in the Ecclesiastical Province of Ontario.

14. Ibid., p. 12.
15. OA, RG 18, MS 164, Scrapbook of Clippings, Timmins *Daily Press*, October 2, 1946, n. p.
16. *LFP*, November 8, 1946.
17. DHA, *Synod Journal*, 1947, p. 66.
18. DHA, WAT papers, Robert Doerr, essay, "On Every Streetcorner in the Diocese", pp. 2-3.
19. DHA, Seager papers, Church Extension file, A Report to the Archbishop from the Committee on Church Extension in London, November 13, 1946.
20. DHA, *Synod Journal*, 1947, p. 36.
21. Ibid., special session, September, 1948.
22. DHA, WAT papers, Doerr essay, p. 26.
23. DHA, WAT papers, Huron College Finance file, Report on the Sale of the Old College. I have withheld the name of the individual involved in this affair.
24. J.J. Talman, op. cit., pp. 89-90.
25. DHA, WAT papers, Huron College Finances file, Townshend to Rev. S.H. Coleman, Westport, Ont., June 2, 1952, pp. 88-90.
26. This episode is recorded in the correspondence, but again I have withheld the person's name.
27. LBE *Minutes*, October 9, 1947, p. 135 and November 13, 1947, p. 149.
28. W.G. Flemming, "Educational Contributions of Associations", *Ontario's Educative Society*, vol. VII (Toronto, 1972), p. 183.
29. *Argus*, vol. 9, no. 11, November, 1950, p. 146.
30. Ibid., p. 146.
31. Ibid., p. 147.
32. Ibid.
33. Ibid.
34. Ibid., inside back cover of the journal.
35. *Ottawa Evening Citizen*, October 24, 1949.
36. Leslie Frost to Harold Hale, June 12, 1951, quoted in Roger Graham, *Old Man Ontario: Leslie M. Frost* (Toronto, 1990), p. 183.
37. C.F. Coulson, op. cit., pp. 385, 388.
38. Ibid., p. 389.
39. DHA, WAT papers, R file, Townshend to P.B. Rice, 77 Northland Crescent, Woodstock, Ont., February 10, 1965.
40. *Report of the Royal Commission*, p. 41.
41. DHA, WAT papers. R file, Townshend to Rice.
42. It is difficult to tell just how influential the London board's brief was on the commission's final report in this matter.
43. Edward E. Stewart, "The 1955 Status of the Recommendations of the Royal Commission on Education in Ontario" (M.A. thesis, University of Wisconson 1956); see especially chapt. 11.

44. DHA, WAT papers, R file, Townshend to Rice. Townshend communicated a similar version to this author in an interview in June, 1985. At that time he still possessed his written copy of the recommendations he and Althouse had discussed.
45. LBE *Minutes*, 1951, pp. 4-5.
46. Ibid., January 11, 1951, p. 6.
47. Ibid., December 13, 1951, p. 212.
48. Ibid., December 13, 1951, p. 213.
49. *Journal of General Synod*, 1952, p. 319.
50. Ibid., p. 405.
51. *LFP*, September 5, 1952, p. 1.
52. DHA, WAT papers, General Synod Budget Committee file, Townshend to Most Rev. L.R. Sherman, Winnipeg, Man., January 3, 1951.
53. DHA, WAT papers, General Synod Budget file, Rt. Rev. Harold Waterman to the Ven. W.A. Townshend, January 15, 1954.
54. DHA, *Synod Journal*, pp. 16-19 and 64-65.
55. *LFP*, September 20, 1955.

CHAPTER FIVE

1. DHA, WAT papers. Bishop Luxton file contains this entire correspondence.
2. DHA, WAT papers. A Christmas Message from the Suffragan Bishop, December, 1955.
3. DHA, WAT papers. Confirmation file contains these letters.
4. Rev. Orlo Miller to the author, July 31, 1986.
5. Rev. Clifford Tomkins to the author, August 11, 1986.
6. Ven. Peter Moore to the author, April 2, 1985.
7. Rev. Canon B.A. Silcox to the author, July 26, 1986.
8. Rev. Maxwell Parker to the author, July 7, 1986. Before moving to Toronto, Parker had been the bursar and a lecturer at Huron College.
9. DHA, *Synod Journal*, 1956. Address of the Suffragan Bishop, p. 41.
10. Ibid., pp. 38-44 and 82-84.
11. *LFP*, May 7, 1957, p. 1.
12. DHA, *Synod Journal*, 1957, p. 101.
13. Ibid.
14. Ibid., pp. 28-30.
15. Ibid., p. 104.
16. DHA, WAT papers, B file, Townshend to Rev. E.F. Bishop, St. Thomas, May 11, 1957.
17. Rev. Canon E.S. Wells to the author, July 17, 1986.
18. DHA, WAT papers, D file, Rt. Rev. A.H. O'Neil, Fredericton, N.B. to Townshend, March 1, 1957 in which O'Neil thanked Townshend for attending and making the presentation.

19. DHA, WAT papers. Rev. T.J. Finlay file contains all the correspondence about this event.
20. DHA, WAT papers, B file, Townshend to Mrs. S.J. Buchanan, Stratford, May 10, 1957.
21. DHA, WAT papers, M file, Townshend to L.A. MacKay, 2505 Woolsey St., Berkeley, Calif., July 23, 1957.
22. UWO, Senate Minutes, October 24, 1958 record that this was the first meeting he had missed in 20 years. Yet a perusal of the minutes shows he had missed many before this one.
23. Ibid., October 25, 1957.
24. For some reason, no inaugural address was recorded in the LBE *Minutes* that year. Only his valedictory speech was retained.
25. Ibid., p. 229.
26. DHA, WAT papers, M file, Mrs. Trueman MacLaughlan, Secretary-Treasurer, Township of Yarmouth School Area 2, St. Thomas, Ont. to Townshend, January 20, 1958 [sic; it should be 1959].
27. DHA, WAT papers, Lambeth Conference file, Bishop G. Luxton to Most Rev. G.F. Fisher, London, Eng., September 20, 1956.
28. Ibid., Townshend to Most Rev. W.F. Barfoot, Winnipeg, Man., June 19, 1957.
29. Ibid., Townshend to Barfoot, February 3, 1958.
30. By coincidence, the author also sailed on that ship, although he and the Bishop did not meet. It was a very cold journey and the author suffered from sea sickness.
31. The full report is printed in *The Report of the Lambeth Conference, 1958* (London, 1958), pp. 99-115.
32. A full account of all aspects of the conference is given in Allan M.G. Stephenson, *Anglicanism and Lambeth Conferences* (London, 1978).
33. DHA, WAT papers, T file, Townshend to Ven. S.F. Tackaberry, Edmonton, Alta., December 18, 1958.
34. HCA, WAT papers. File of Speeches and Sermons, Address to the Public School Trustees Association of Ontario, October 21, 1958.
35. Ibid.
36. HCA, WAT papers, Public School Trustees file, Reg. W. Kennedy, secretary, London Diocesan Trustees Association to Rt. Rev. Wm. Townshend, October 28, 1958. The letter simply contained the resolution without any commentary. It ended with the sentence, "This resolution is based on a current newspaper report of a few days ago."
37. DHA, WAT papers, Public School Trustees file, Townshend to Rev. J.V. Mills, January 21, 1958.
38. *LFP*, December 11, 1958 and the programme for the Official Opening of Bishop Townshend Public School, Wednesday, December 10, 1958. This document was lent to the author by the Bishop.

39. DHA, *Synod Journal*, 1963, p. 111. The material in the above paragraphs has been drawn from his annual reports to Synod printed in the journals for the years 1959 to 1963.
40. DHA, *Synod Journal*, 1960, pp. 131-135. The Report of the Committee to Study Future Policy of the Diocese.
41. Ibid., p. 133.
42. DHA, WAT papers. File on Future of the Diocese, Statement read by Bishop Townshend to a sub-committee of the Committee to Study the Future Policy of the Diocese on January 29, 1960.
43. DHA, *Synod Journal*, 1960, pp. 133-134.
44. Ibid., p. 51.
45. The Bishop once told the author that President Hall actually ordered him to stay away from a senate meeting so that body could pass the necessary resolution.
46. *LFP*, June 6, 1960, p. 3.
47. See J.W. Grant, op. cit., chapt. 9 for a discussion of the impact of these trends upon the Canadian churches.
48. See R.M. Stamp, op. cit., especially chapt. 10 for a general description of these developments.
49. DHA, WAT papers, L file, Townshend to Rev. Canon H.M. Langford, Waterloo, Ont., February 22, 1961.
50. Orlo Miller, *This Was London* (London, Ont., 1988), p. 210.
51. Only one other person, C.C. Carrothers, ever held this position more often, and he was elected seven times.
52. LBE *Minutes*, January 18, 1962, pp. 3-10.
53. Ibid., pp. 5-6.
54. Ibid., p. 10.
55. Ibid., pp. 362-363.
56. Ibid., p. 363.
57. Ibid.
58. For a good description of the emergence of the Reorganized Programme see R.M. Stamp, op. cit., pp. 203-206 and V.K. Gilbert, *Let Each Become* (Toronto, 1972), chapt. 22.
59. For a discussion of its decline see V.K. Gilbert, op. cit., chapts. 4 and 5 and John Stapleton, "The Politics of Educational Innovation" (Ph.D. diss., University of Toronto 1975), pp. 11-12.
60. LBE *Minutes*, 1962, p. 363.
61. Ibid., p. 238. This name had been applied to all of London's collegiate institutes and vocational schools as a result of a board decision taken on June 21, 1962. Townshend voted against the adoption of this title but the minutes do not indicate his reasons.
62. Ibid., p. 365.
63. Ibid., p. 366.
64. Franklin Walker, op. cit., vol. III, chapt. 5. This is the most detailed account of this episode.

65. The full text of the bishops' brief is contained in J. Bascom St. John, *Separate Schools in Ontario* (Toronto, 1963), pp. 29-40.
66. HCA, WAT papers. File, Roman Catholic Bishops' Brief, contains a copy of the *Memorandum Presented by the Anglican Bishops of Ontario to the Prime Minister and Members of the Provincial Legislature*, 6 pp. It is dated December 12, 1962, which is the day the bishops had their interview with Premier Robarts. Obviously, the document had been prepared earlier.
67. DHA, HCA. There is no information in Townshend's papers about this meeting. See *Globe and Mail*, December 13, 1962, p. 1. There is a photograph of a very glum looking Premier surrounded by the four bishops. See also *LFP*, December 13, 1962, p. 1.
68. HCA, WAT papers, Public School Trustees file, Townshend to Mr. L.H. Saunders, Toronto, May 30, 1962.
69. Ibid.
70. Ibid.
71. D.C. Cameron, *The Schools of Ontario* (Toronto, 1972), chapt. 4.
72. HCA, WAT papers, T file, Townshend to the Rev. G.R. Thompson, 27 Ash Grove Place, Don Mills, Ont., May 22, 1962.
73. DHA, WAT papers, J file, Townshend to Rev. T.D. Jones, 1450 Union Ave, Montreal, P.Q., June 19, 1963.
74. DHA, WAT papers. File, General Synod Pension Plan Committee Reports, Report of the Pension Plan Commission, signed by Townshend, J.C. Osler, Q.C. and J.H. Moore, F.C.A., May 27, 1959, p. 1.
75. Ibid., Archbishop W. Barfoot to Townshend, March 14, 1958.
76. Ibid., Townshend to Barfoot, March 29, 1958.
77. Ibid., Barfoot to Townshend, April 7, 1958.
78. Ibid., Townshend to Rt. Rev. S.C. Steer, January 29, 1960.
79. Ibid., Townshend to Bishop Steer, March 4, 1960, and Townshend to Archbishop Clark, March 15, 1960.
80. Ibid., Townshend to Bishop Frederick Wilkinson, June 1, 1960.
81. Ibid. Copy of his Address re: presentation of the Report of the Primate's Pension Plan Commission, House of Bishops, Oakville, Ont., August 26, 1960.
82. HCA, WAT papers, Primate file, Townshend to Most Rev. H.H. Clark, Winnipeg, Man., April 3, 1963.
83. E.R. Fairweather, ed., *Anglican Congress 1963: Report of the Proceedings* (Toronto, 1963).
84. HCA, WAT papers. File, Bilingual and Bicultural Commission, General Remarks, 4 pp., June 6, 1964. There are two copies of his comments in this file.
85. Ibid. All the quotations in this paragraph are drawn from the General Remarks.
86. DHA, *Synod Journal*, 1965, p. 171.
87. Actually, this idea was never adopted.

88. DHA, *Synod Journal*, 1965, p. 96.
89. DHA, WAT papers, H file, Townshend to Rev. H.B. Hamilton, 251 W. 80th St., New York, 24, N.Y., March 22, 1966.
90. Ibid., D file, Townshend to Most Rev. A.H. O'Neil, M.A., D.D., D.C.L., 791 Brunswick St., Fredericton, N.B., July 16, 1965.
91. DHA, WAT papers, M file, Townshend to Mr. & Mrs. Alfred Moreton, 17 Ford Blvd., Windsor, Ont., September 23, 1966; Townshend to Mr. & Mrs. George Macarthur, 43 Humbercrest Blvd., Toronto, Ont., Sept. 28, 1966.
92. HCA, WAT papers, J file, Townshend to Rev. T.D. Jones, L.Th., 1450 Union Ave., Montreal, P.Q., May 24, 1966.
93. Ibid., p. 77. There may have been some confusion in the use of 50 year time span in this resolution. He had been ordained in 1926, and thus had served only 40 years in the ministry, but he had preached his first sermon 50 years earlier.
94. Ibid.
95. *LFP*, December 6, 1966, p. A1.
96. Ibid., p. B2.
97. Ibid.

CHAPTER SIX

1. DHA, WAT papers, Confirmation file, Townshend to Rt. Rev. G.B. Snell, M.A., Ph.D., D.D., 135 Adelaide St. E., Toronto 1, Ont., February 10, 1967.
2. Ibid.
3. Ibid., Townshend to Miss Joan Cloke, secretary to Bishop Snell, 135 Adelaide St. E., Toronto 1, Ont., March 7, 1967.
4. Ibid., Townshend to the Rt. Rev. G.B. Snell, February 10, 1967.
5. Ibid. There are approximately 20 letters dealing with this tour. Once again, Townshend's and the author's paths crossed. One of the churches where he held a confirmation was St. Paul's, Newmarket, whose rector was Rev. Canon J.T. Rhodes. The author was a parishioner of Canon Rhodes at the time.
6. Ibid., Townshend to Mrs. Fred Ritchie, 61 Stone St., Elmvale, Ont., March 30, 1967.
7. Ibid., Townshend to Rt. Rev. G.B. Snell, May 5, 1967.
8. Ibid., Townshend to Snell, May 5, 1967. This date is obviously incorrect as the last service on his submitted list was given as May 17, St. Margaret's West Hill. Yet he simply put a question mark in the column for the number of persons confirmed, whereas he inserted specific numbers for all the other parishes.
9. Ibid., Townshend to Rev. C.H. Groh, St. John's Episcopal Church, 33 East Montcalm St., Detroit 1, Michigan, April 14, 27, 30, 1967.

10. Ibid., April 27, 1967.
11. Ibid., Townshend to Snell, June 1, 1967.
12. Since his official correspondence stopped at the end of these confirmation services in 1967, it is virtually impossible to trace all of the services and events in various parishes which he undertook for the rest of his life.
13. LBE *Minutes*, 1967, pp. 442, 632.
14. Ibid., p. 148 and information supplied by Mr. Tom Moore, Executive Secretary of the London Board of Education, May 15, 1989.
15. V.K. Gilbert, op. cit., p. 51.
16. *Living and Learning* (Toronto, 1968), p. 38.
17. For a complete discussion of the workings of this committee and of the "politics" of the credit system see John Stapleton, op. cit.
18. OA, R.G. 2 Acc. 10049, Box 2, Brief A-77, Brief Submitted to the Provincial Committee on Aims and Objectives in Education by the Board of Education For the City of London, 12 pp., January 7, 1966.
19. LBE *Minutes*, 1969, pp. 495-496.
20. *LFP*, December 2, 1969, p. A8.
21. This description was given to me by Mr. R. Mann, a former secondary-school principal.
22. LBE *Minutes*, 1971, p. 380. The full report is printed on pp. 379-385.
23. Ibid., p. 385.
24. *LFP*, February 18, 1972, p. A1.
25. Ibid.
26. LBE *Minutes*, 1972, p. 85.
27. LBE *Minutes*, 1975, pp. 39-40.
28. Ibid., pp. 72-75.
29. Press Release, District 4 Ontario Secondary School Teachers' Federation, 1978 06 01.
30. *LFP*, July 13, 1979 and *Western News*, July 12, 1979.
31. LBE *Minutes*, October 7, 1980, p. 24.
32. Ibid., pp. 24-25.
33. Ibid., p. 25.
34. *London Tribune*, October 16, 1980, p. 3.
35. *LFP*, Monday, November 24, 1980, p. A16. Also, the brochure prepared by Tom Moore, *In Honour of Service*, November 22, 1980, n.p. The Bishop lent the author an autographed copy belonging originally to the Hon. Gordon Walker, which has Walker's notes for his speech on the front cover.
36. *LFP*, September 13, 1984.
37. *LFP*, November 30, 1985.
38. DHA, WAT papers, Townshend to Mr. Monte Anions, General Hospital, Chatham, Ont., August 23, 1966.
39. *LFP*, January 21, 1988.

Bibliography

PRIMARY SOURCES

Manuscripts

¤ Church of the Redeemer Archives, London, Ontario:

Vestry Minute Book, 1926-1947
Minutes of the Select Vestry
Minute Book of the Deanery of East Middlesex
Invitations to the Annual Parish Fairs, 1930-1938
Miscellaneous Documents

¤ Diocese of Huron Archives, Huron College, the University of Western Ontario, London, Ontario. The transcripts of the taped interviews of Bishop Townshend made by William Townshend and Susan Townshend have been deposited here by the author. This archive also holds the papers and correspondence of the following bishops:

Rt. Rev. George Luxton, 1948-1970
Most Rev. C.A. Seager, 1932-1948
Rt. Rev. W.A.T. Townshend, 1939-1967
Most Rev. David Williams, 1904-1931
Minutes of the Executive Committee of the Diocese of Huron, 1938-1967
Files of the Diocesan Commissioner, 1939-1947
Journals of the Diocesan Synod of Huron, 1926-1967
Preacher's Book, Parish of Bervie, Bervie, Ontario

¤ Diocese of Huron, Synod Office, London, Ontario: Journals of the General Synod of the Anglican Church of Canada

¤ Huron College Archives, Huron College, the University of Western Ontario, London, Ontario: Minutes of the College Council, 1934-1971.

¤ Archives of the Province of Ontario:

R.G.2 Acc.10049 Box 2, Brief A-77, Brief Submitted to the Provincial Committee on the Aims and Objectives of Education by the Board of Education for the City of London, 12 pp. January 7, 1966.

R.G.18 Commissions and Committees, Royal Commission on Education in Ontario (December 15, 1950), Proceedings, Volume 1, B-115, Box 1.

R.G.18 Ms 164 Scrapbook of Clippings concerning the Royal Commission on Education in Ontario.

¤ The University of Western Ontario, Regional History Room, Weldon Library, London, Ontario: the University of Western Ontario calendars, 1917-1919.

¤ The University of Western Ontario, Senate Office: Senate Minutes, 1936-1967.

Printed Documents

In Honour of Service, booklet for the banquet honouring the Rt. Rev. W.A. Townshend, Saturday, November 22, 1980.

Minutes of the Board of Education for the City of London, 1934-1980.

Official Opening of the Bishop Townshend Public School, December 10, 1958.

Report of the Royal Commission on Education in Ontario, Toronto, King's Printer, 1950.

Interviews

- Susan Townshend and Rt. Rev. W.A. Townshend.
- William Townshend and Rt. Rev. W.A. Townshend.

Letters to the Author

From A.L. Crich, May Boyle, Rev. Orlo Miller, Rev. Clifford Tomkins, Ven. Peter Moore, Rev. Canon B.A. Silcox, Rev. Dr. Max Parker, Rev. Canon E.S. Wells.

Newspapers and Magazines

London Free Press
London Argus
London Tribune
Ottawa Evening Citizen
Globe and Mail
Huron Church News
Western News
Daily Press (Timmins)

SECONDARY SOURCES

Books

Armstrong, F.H. *The Forest City, An Illustrated History of London.* Windsor (Ontario): Windsor Publications Ltd., 1986.

Barzun, Jacques. *Clio and the Doctors: Psycho-History, Quanto-History and History*. Chicago: University of Chicago Press, 1974.

Cameron, D.C. *The Schools of Ontario*. Toronto: University of Toronto Press, 1972.

Carrington, Philip. *The Anglican Church in Canada*. Toronto: Collins, 1963.

Crowley, Terry. *Clios' Craft. A Primer of Historical Methods*. Toronto: Copp Clark Pitman, 1988.

Edel, Leon. *Writing Lives: Principia Biographica*. New York: W.W. Norton, 1984.

Edel, Leon and Marc Pachter. *Telling Lives*. Washington: New Republic Books, 1979.

Epstein, William H. *Recognizing Biography*. Philadelphia: University of Pennsylvania Press, 1987.

Fairweather, E.R., ed. *Anglican Congress 1963, Report of the Proceedings*. Toronto: Anglican Book Centre, 1963.

Flemming, W.G. *Ontario's Educative Society*, 8 vols. Toronto: University of Toronto Press, 1972.

Gilbert, V.K. *Let Each Become*. Toronto: Guidance Centre, Faculty of Education, University of Toronto, 1972.

Graham, Roger. *Old Man Ontario: Leslie M. Frost*. Toronto: University of Toronto, 1990.

Grant, John Webster. *The Church in the Canadian Era*, 1st ed. Toronto: McGraw-Hill Ryerson, 1972.

Homberger, Eric and John Charmley, eds. *The Troubled Face of Biography*. New York: St. Martin's Press, 1988.

Living and Learning: Report of the Provincial Committee on Aims and Objectives of Education in Ontario. Toronto: Newton Publishing, 1968.

McHenty, Neil. *Mitch Hepburn*. Toronto: McClelland & Stewart, 1976.

Miller, Orlo. *This Was London*. Westport (Ontario): Butternut Press, 1988.

Nadel, Ira Bruce. *Biography: Fact, Fiction and Forum*. London and Basingstoke: Macmillan, 1984.

Novarr, David. *The Lines of Life: Theories of Biography, 1880-1970*. West Lafayette (Indiana): Purdue University Press, 1986.

Pulker, Edward. *We Stand On Their Shoulders*. Toronto: Anglican Book Centre, 1986.

The Report of the Lambeth Conference, 1958. London: S.P.C.K. and Seabury Press, 1958.

Runyan, William McKinley. *Life Histories and Psychobiography*. New York: Oxford University Press, 1982.

Sidelsky, Robert. "Only Connect: Biography and Truth", in Homberger, Eric and John Charmley, eds., *The Troubled Face of Biography*. New York: St. Martin's Press, 1988.

St. John, J. Bascom. *Separate Schools in Ontario*. Toronto: Globe and Mail Press, 1963.

Stamp, R.M. *The Schools of Ontario*. Toronto: University of Toronto Press, 1982.

Stannard, David. *Shrinking History: On Freud and the Failure of Psychology*. New York: Oxford University Press, 1980.

Stephenson, M.G. *Anglicans and Lambeth Conferences*. London: S.P.C.K., 1978.

Talman, J.J. *Huron College*. London, Ont., 1963.

Tuchman, Barbara. "Biography as a Prism of History", in Leon Edel and Marc Pachter, *Telling Lives*. Washington: New Republic Books, 1979.

Walker, Franklin. *Catholic Education and Politics in Ontario*. Toronto: Catholic Education Foundation of Ontario, 1986.

West, Francis. *Biography as History*. Sydney: Sydney University Press for the Australian Academy of the Humanities, 1973.

Woolf, Virginia. "The Art of Biography", in *Collected Works*, vol. 14. New York: Harcourt, Brace and World, 1967.

Theses

Coulson, C.F. "An Historical Survey of Royal Commissions and Other Major Government Investigations in Education", Ed.D. diss., University of Toronto, 1956.

Stapleton, John. "The Politics of Educational Innovation", Ph.D. dissertation, University of Toronto, 1975.

Stewart, Edward E. "The 1955 Status of the Recommendations in the Report of the Royal Commission on Education in Ontario", M.A. thesis, University of Wisconsin, 1956.

Index

ALTHOUSE, J.G., 80
Anglican Advance Appeal, 55, 68-69
Anglican Book Centre, 93
Anglican Forward Movement, 22
Anions, Monte, 155n
Appleyard, Archdeacon Harold, 104
Armstrong, F.H., 144n
Auden, W.H., 1

BAGNELL, RT. REV. W., 99
Barfoot, Most Rev. W., 83, 84, 98, 116-117, 151n, 153n
Barry, Rt. Rev. F.R., 99
Barzun, Jacques, 144n
Bayfield, 7, 10, 13, 18, 33, 94, 96, 119, 124, 128, 129, 131, 139
Beal, H.B., 27, 35
Beal Technical School, 31
Sir Adam Beck Collegiate Institute, 35
Bervie, Kingarf and Kinlough, 19, 24
Bishop Townshend Public School, 102, 150n, 151n
Book of Common Prayer, 16, 21, 55, 90, 92
Boswell, James, 2
Bothwell, Most Rev. John, 140
Boyle, May, 145n
Bradfield, Rt. Rev. H.W., 99
Brescia College, 52, 97, 147n
Briggs, Bruce, 144n
Brown, Robert Craig, 144n
Buchanan, S.J., 151n
Buchner, William (Bill), 124
Budget Committee, 83-84

CAMERON, D.C., 153n
Careless, J.M.S., 3
Carrington, Philip, 145n, 148n
Carrothers, C.C., 30, 37, 51, 113, 124, 152n
Chalmers, M.W., 108
Charmley, John, 2, 143n
Church Extension Committee, 69, 93-95, 102-103, 122
Church of the Redeemer, 24-40 *passim*, 73, 122
Church of St. John the Evangelist, 25, 85
Clark, Greg, 105
Clark, Most Rev. H. H., 119, 153n
Clinton, 8, 139, 140
Cloke, Joan, 154n
Cody, Most Rev. John, 116
Cody, Rev. Canon Henry, 37
Coleman, Rt. Rev. Michael, 106-107
Coleman, Rev. S.H., 73, 149n
Coleman, Rt. Rev. W., 73,
Conservative Party, 37-39, 54
Confirmation Services, 92-93
Conron, A.B., 97
Coulson, C.F., 148n, 149n
Council for Social Service, 21
Creighton, D.G., 3
Crich, A.L., 144n, 159n
Crowley, Terry, 144n

DAVIS, PREMIER WILLIAM G., 138
Dennis, Lloyd, 129

Department of Education, 105, 106, 109-112, 114, 129, 132, 133
Diefenbaker, John George, 17, 110
Diocesan Forward Campaign, 57, 58, 68
Diocesan Trustees Association of the Roman Catholic Diocese of London, 101
Doerr, Robert, 149n
Doherty, Archdeacon W.I., 70
Drew, Premier George, 54, 63, 147n
DuMoulin, P., 117
Duncan, Dr. A.S., 38

EDEL, LEON, 2, 3, 4, 143n, 144n
Elborn College, 109
Elston, Rev. M.H., 46
Elton, Sir Geoffrey, 1
Every Member Canvass, 46

FAIRWEATHER, E.R., 153n
Finlay, Rev. T.J., 96
Fisher, Most Rev. G., 98
Flemming, W.G., 149n
Ford, Arthur, 105
Forward Commission, 56-57
Foster, Rev. Canon Robert, 140
French, Dr. Stanley, 129
Frost, Premier Leslie, 77, 149n

GENERAL BOARD OF RELIGIOUS EDUCATION, 21
General Synod, 21, 22, 46, 68, 83-85, 86-88, 93, 116-120, 153n
General Synod Pension Commission, 108-111
Gilbert, V.K., 152, 155n
Given, J.D., 108
Graham, Roger, 149n
Grant, John Webster, 22, 61-62, 145n, 152n
Gray, Rt. Rev. Walter, 99
Groh, Rev. C.H., 128, 155n
Guest, Rev. Duncan, 16

HALL-DENNIS COMMITTEE, 78, 129-132
Hall-Dennis Report (*Living and Learning*), 129-132, 133, 135, 136, 155n
Hall, Mr. Justice Emmett, 129
Hamill, Gordon, 117-118
Hamilton, Rev. H.B., 122, 154n
Hardy, Madeleine, 138
Harrison, Evelyn, 65
Hepburn, Premier Mitchell, 31, 32, 38
Homberger, Eric, 2, 143n
Honour, Rev. G.S., 145n
Hope, Mr. Justice John, 62, 65, 111
Hunt, Rt. Rev. H.R., 107
Huron College, 4, 14, 15-17, 26, 72-73, 97, 106-107
Huron, Diocese of, 23, 39, 41, 48-49, 50, 69, 83 *passim*

JEAKINS, REV. C.E., 13
Jennings, Rev. E.C., 94
Jones, Rt. Rev. Derwyn, 140
Jones, Rev. T.D., 153n, 154n

KENNEDY, R.W., 151n
Kilbourn, William, 3
Kingsmill, Fred, 30, 37

LAMBETH CONFERENCE, 98-100, 120
Lampman, Ralph, 144n
Lamp of Learning Award, 96
Langford, Rev. Canon H. M., 152n
London Board of Education, *passim*
London Normal School, 101, 109
Lawson, Hon. Ray, 74
Lawson, Tom, 30
Luxton, Rt. Rev. George, 70, 71, 72, 85, 86, 88, 89, 91, 93, 98, 102-104, 120, 122, 151n

MANILLA, 18-19, 127
Mann, R., 155n
McAlister, F.C., 59

Macarthur, Mr. & Mrs. George, 154n
McHenty, Neil, 145n
MacKay, J. Keiller, 133
MacKay Report, 133-134
MacKay Louis, 96, 151n
MacLaughlan, Mrs. Trueman, 151n
McNaught, Kenneth, 3
Middlesex College, 97
Miller, Rev. Orlo, 150n, 152n, 159n
Mills, Archdeacon, J.H.N., 86
Mills, Rev. J.V., 102, 151n
Missionary Society of the Canadian Church, 46, 88, 93
Montgomery-Campbell, Rt. Rev. H.C., 99
Moore, J.H. (Jake), 117, 153n
Moore, Ven. Peter, 150n
Moore, Tom, 139, 155n
Morden, Archdeacon John Grant, 106-107, 116, 141
Moreton, Mr. & Mrs. Alfred, 154n

NAMIER, SIR LEWIS, 1
Nimmo, Rev. Alexander, 104
Novarr, David, 2, 143n

O'DRISCOLL, RT. REV. PERCY, 140
O'Neil, Most Rev. Henry, 48, 69, 72, 95, 98, 122, 150n, 154n
Ontario College of Education, 109
Ontario Secondary School Teachers' Federation, 36, 81, 96, 137, 155n
Orange Lodge, 31, 37
Osler, John, 117, 153n
Owen, Most Rev. Derwyn, 46

PARKER, REV. MAXWELL, 93, 150n, 159n
Peers, Most Rev. Michael, 140
Perkins, Rev. Handley, 147n
Primatial See Committee, 83-84
Property Committee, 60, 102, 120
Provincial Synod, 67, 114
Public School Trustees Association of Ontario, 74-76, 100, 102
Pulker, Edward, 147n

QU'APPELLE, DIOCESE OF, 17
Queen, Archdeacon Cameron, 106

REORGANIZED PROGRAMME, 109-113, 152n
Rhodes, Rev. Canon, J.T., 154n
Rice, P.B., 149n, 150n
Ritchie, Mrs. Fred, 128, 154n
Rivers, F.W., 102
Robarts, Premier John P., 109, 112, 114, 153n
Robinson, Rt. Rev. C.C., 99
Roman Catholics, 31-32, 37, 74-75, 77, 95, 101, 113-116
Rowe, Earl, 38
Rowe, Rev. J.G., 106
Royal Commission on Bilingualism and Biculturalism, 120-121
Royal Commission on Education in Ontario, 59, 62-63, 64, 65-66, 70, 76, 81, 130, 131, 132, 141, 148n, 149n
Ruch, Rev. R.A.E., 147n
Ryerson, Egerton, 37

ST. ANDREW'S MEMORIAL CHURCH, 70
St. Jacques, Henry, 76
St. John, J. Bascom, 153n
Saunders, L.H., 153n
Schoales, R.D., 102
Scotchmere, Alfred George, grandfather of WAT, 8
Seager, Most Rev. Charles, 39-40, 41, 42, 45, 48, 49, 50, 58, 59, 70, 71, 79, 146n, 148n, 149n
Secondary School Curriculum, 29-30, 35-36, 51-53, 64, 66, 67, 79, 109-113, 131, 141
Sewell, Very Rev. William, 106

Sherman, Most. Rev. L.R., 150n
Silcox, Rev. Canon B.A., 150n, 159n
Skidelsky, Robert, 1, 143n
Sloman, Fred, 13
Snell, Rt. Rev. George, 127-128, 154n
Snowden, Archdeacon J.M., 146n
Stamp, R.M., 45, 145n, 146n, 148n, 152n
Stannard, David E., 144n
Stapleton, John, 152n, 155n
Steer, Rt. Rev. S.C., 117-118, 153n
Stephenson, Allan M.G., 151n
Stewart, E.E., 149n
Strachey, Lytton, 2-3, 143n
Sutton, W.D., 108

TACKABERRY, VEN. S.F., 151n
Talman, J.J., 144n, 149n
Technical and Vocational Training Assistance Act (1960), 110, 113
Thomas, Rev. Canon A. Brant, 107
Thompson, Rev. G.R., 153n
Thompson, Rev. John, 128
Tomkins, Rev. Clifford, 150n, 159n
Townshend, Bishop William Alfred, *passim*
Townshend, Albert, father, 7, 8, 9, 13
Townshend, Alvin, brother, 7, 144n
Townshend, Betty, daughter, 57
Townshend, Eleanor, daughter, 19, 57, 122, 123, 124
Townshend, Eleanor, grandmother, 8
Townshend, Eleanor, sister, 7
Townshend, Ernest, brother, 7, 11, 144n
Townshend, Hannah (*née* Scotchmere), mother, 7, 8, 13
Townshend, John, brother, 7, 47, 108, 144n
Townshend, John, son, 19, 26, 47, 57, 108, 144n
Townshend, Kathleen (*née* Elliott), wife, 9, 10, 11, 12, 14, 18, 19, 24, 37, 47, 57, 58, 70, 89, 94, 98, 119, 127-128, 137, 139, 140
Townshend, Rev. Peter, grandson, 139, 140
Townshend, Robert, son, 39, 47, 116, 139-140
Townshend, Susan, granddaughter, 144n *passim*
Townshend, William, grandfather, 7, 8, 9,
Townshend, William, son, 19, 26-27, 57, 144n *passim*
Townshend Medal, i, 137
Trumper, Rev. Canon A.A., 70

VOCATIONAL ADVISORY COMMITTEE, 31, 52, 134

WALKER, FRANKLIN, 145n, 152n
Walker, Hon. Gordon, 138, 155n
Waller, Rev. C.C., 15, 48, 132
Waterman, Rt. Rev. R.H., 87, 150n
Wells, Rev. Canon E.S., 150n, 159n
West, Francis, 1, 143n
Western Ontario, University of, 14, 36, 51, 52, 97, 104, 137
Wheable, G.A., 28, 52, 65, 66
Wilkey, Dr. John, 44
Wilkinson, Rt. Rev. F.H., 90, 114, 118, 153n
Williams, Most Rev. David, 17, 24, 157n
Woolf, Virginia, 1, 6
World War One, 4, 12, 16
World War Two, 44-45, 53, 54, 55, 62
Wright, Most Rev. W.L., 90, 114